NAPOLEON HILL'S

first editions

ON MASTERING PERSONAL AND PROFESSIONAL SUCCESS

ACTIONS AND ANNOTATIONS BY ENTREPRENEUR MEDIA

Entrepreneur Press®

Entrepreneur Press, Publisher

Cover Design: Andrew Welyczko

Production and Composition: Ponderosa Pine Design

© 2020 by Entrepreneur Media, Inc.

Entrepreneur Press® is a registered trademark of Entrepreneur Media, Inc.

An application to register this book for cataloging has been submitted to the Library of Congress.

Printed in the United States of America

25 24 23 22 21   10 9 8 7 6 5 4 3 2 1

Contents

Foreword

Don M. Green, Executive Director
of Napoleon Hill Foundation

Napoleon Hill was born in 1883 in the mountains of Southwest Virginia in a two-room cabin in an area that was noted for three things—feuds, moonshine, and ignorant people. In an unpublished autobiography, Hill reflecting on his childhood said, "For three generations my people had been born, lived, struggled in ignorance and poverty, and died without having been outside the mountains of that section." Hill often mentioned those early years of his life in his articles, speeches, and books.

Being born in a remote area with very few opportunities for success, Napoleon had experienced the tragedy of losing his mother when he was only 9 years old. Within one year after the loss of his mother, Napoleon's father remarried and Hill's stepmother quickly took a liking to him and saw his potential. Napoleon's stepmother was educated—the daughter of a doctor and the widow of a school principal. She encouraged Napoleon to write and while still a teenager, he was turning out simple news items.

Napoleon finished a local two-year high school and made the decision to attend a business school. His desire was to become a male secretary (what we would now refer to as an administrative assistant). Upon completion of the business school, Hill wrote General Rufus Ayres for a job—probably because of Ayres' wealth. Ayres, a lawyer by profession was a true entrepreneur, having his own banking business, coal business, and lumber business. Hill went to work for Ayres and his new passion was to become a lawyer.

Napoleon convinced his brother, Vivian, to apply to Georgetown Law School. Hill, an eternal optimist, told Vivian that he would support both of them and he got a job writing for a magazine owned by Bob Taylor, former governor of Tennessee and a United States senator. Writing success stories compiled from Hill's earlier interviews would define his life's work.

One of Napoleon Hill's first interviews was with Andrew Carnegie. Andrew Carnegie was an interesting study in success principles. He came to the United States as a 12-year-old and with very little education. Carnegie had advanced quickly and by the age of 35, he was one of the country's empire builders. Combining various steel makers into a conglomerate in the form of U.S. Steel, Carnegie amassed a fortune.

Hill was excited listening to Carnegie talk on the "Principles of Achievement." Carnegie saw his humble origins as an inspiration to overcome all obstacles and attain worthy goals. He explained to Hill that the starting point for success was definiteness of purpose.

Carnegie challenged Hill to complete an assignment of the study of great leaders, compile the information, compose it, and make it available to others as a tool to help them. Hill accepted his challenge and while Carnegie furnished no salary, he did a more important deed of providing Hill contacts with America's greatest men.

Napoleon Hill's Magazine and the *Golden Rule Magazine* articles give a glimpse of Hill's future books. When Hill's first book, *Law of Success,* was published in 1928, it was a great success—paying the author up to $3,000 per month, which was a lot of money nearly 100 years ago.

In 1937, Hill was to complete the book *Think and Grow Rich* which continues to sell hundreds of thousands of copies each year worldwide. *Think and Grow Rich* has a following of devout individuals who realize its philosophy-of-success message is as relevant today as when it was first written. The book was so well received that it was published three times its first year and sold at $2.50 a copy—this, despite the fact the country was in the middle of the Great Depression. This was before mass media and marketing that is available today.

Hill continued to communicate success principles via radio programs in the 1940s at Warner Brothers Studio in Hollywood and later at WGN TV in Chicago. He continued leading seminars, giving lectures, and making personal appearances, and, finally, he founded the non-profit Napoleon Hill Foundation to spread the principles of success throughout the world. Though Napoleon Hill died in 1970 at the age of 87, his writings are more popular than ever.

Let Hill's book, enhanced by annotations, tips, and additional content from the business experts at Entrepreneur, give you a greater understanding of the length and breadth of Hill's work. Whether you are a student of books like *Law of Success, Think and Grow Rich,* or his other bestsellers, or this is your first book of Napoleon Hill, you will gain insight that will be invaluable.

Introduction

By the Editors of Entrepreneur

When Napoleon Hill began writing about success, he might not have realized the impact his work would have on future generations of writers, thinkers, and the business world. Those initial interviews and subsequent articles and essays are the basis for much of what we read about the topic of success today, and for good reason. They are evergreen concepts that age well. Pick up any book about success and you'll see reverberations of Hill's writings on habits, success, negotiation, and treating colleagues with respect. Hill's foundational knowledge of what success can look like remains strong today.

No matter how you define it, we all seek success in one form or another. And the journey to find it can be long and often daunting. We hope for quick solutions; we don't often find them. We set our goals; often, too high. We depend on others to lay out a path toward success for us; but it's not on them to do so. Ultimately, we find that the true key to success lies within.

Napoleon Hill knew this. He knew that success was entirely dependent on one singular element: you. How you navigate the world and how you treat others is the basis for your own success both in business and in life.

HOW TO USE THIS BOOK

The selections in this book from Napoleon Hill's timeless first writings run the gamut from inspirational to practical. As you read, keep in mind that each essay is a product of its time and place. As such, some language usage and sentence construction may seem unfamiliar to you. We have opted to retain as much of the original tone and voice of the author as possible, providing some updates for modern sensibilities, including headings to help you navigate the content. Our editors have also included some brief editorial comments as needed, which are denoted in brackets.

Each selection includes tips for the reader from our editors, and an "Entrepreneur Action Item" section to help you apply the lesson from each of Hill's original essays to your own life and experience in a practical, actionable way. At the end of the book, you'll find a brief reader's guide packed with thought-provoking questions that you can use in your reading group, class, or even for yourself to keep the conversation on success going.

HARNESS THE POWER OF YOU

Hill famously said, "All the breaks you need in life wait within your imagination . . . . Imagination is the workshop of your mind, capable of turning mind energy into accomplishments and wealth." So, what are you waiting for? Use your imagination to broaden your own idea of success. Think about what YOU want your life to look like. Do you want to grow in your position at work as a solopreneur? Perhaps you want to forge a path outside the confines of your office and break out on your own as an entrepreneur. Maybe you want to create a passive income that will allow you to focus more on family and fun. Or, perhaps you want to focus on nonwork-related success: quality time with your family, honoring your interests and passions, or even having more time to volunteer and change your corner of the world. Success can look any way you want it to—all it takes is your imagination and the drive to make it happen. Let's get started!

CHAPTER ONE

What You Need to Know

The first thing you need to know is how to make sense of the opening passage of Napoleon Hill's first story, "The End of the Rainbow." Hill introduces this article with a statement that would have been completely understood by his loyal readers at the time, but will leave modern readers scratching their heads.

Hill begins with the somewhat grandiose announcement that this story is going to be a retelling of the dramatic turning points in the previous 12 years of his life. Then, in the very next sentence, he says that he isn't going to tell everything because he has been warned by his friends to leave out the final part of the story. What is he talking about?

The answer is that he's talking about a scandal that took place a year earlier, and to appreciate why this is important to him, you must first know that *Napoleon Hill's Magazine* in which this article appeared, was not Hill's first magazine. It was his second, and the scandal that is so cryptically referred to involves his ouster as publisher of the first one.

The first magazine was called *Hill's Golden Rule* and it was born in Napoleon Hill's mind on Armistice Day, November 11, 1918. The end of the World War so inspired Hill that he vowed that day to create a new magazine to promote the philosophy of the Golden Rule in personal achievement and business success. He found a printer who shared his vision, and they published the first edition in January 1919. It was an instant success.

To Hill, it seemed that this magazine was the fulfillment of everything he had dreamed of and worked for. It gave him a national platform for the secrets of success he had learned from his years of researching the most successful people in America, and it allowed him to teach the lessons he had learned from his own business triumphs and failures. *Hill's Golden Rule* was in every way an extension of him, his talent, his philosophy, and his passion.

Then in the late summer of 1920, Napoleon Hill discovered that his partner had gone behind his back and tried to seize control of the magazine. At first, the partner offered to pay Hill if he would sign an agreement promising to get out of publishing. Hill refused. But when the October issue came out, he saw that his name had been removed from the masthead.

He was devastated for about a month—then he got mad. Then he got even.

Within two months, Hill moved from Chicago to New York City and raised enough money to launch a new publication, *Napoleon Hill's Magazine*. The first issue hit the stands in April, and by the time "The End of the Rainbow" article appeared in the September issue, it was clear that he had accomplished the almost unheard-of feat of launching a magazine that would be profitable in its first year.

The publication of this article marked the one-year anniversary of Napoleon Hill being removed from *Hill's Golden Rule*, which explains why Hill was being so cryptic when he wrote the opening passage to "The End of the Rainbow."

Chapter 3, "A Personal Inventory," is reprinted from the December

1919 issue of *Hill's Golden Rule*. In the story, you will see a familiar word spelled in an unfamiliar way: *kultur*. At the time Hill wrote this story, it had been barely a year since the end of the World War, and kultur was a term that appeared often in newspaper stories during the war with Germany. To the German elite, *kultur* meant their sense of national pride and belief in Germany's natural superiority over other people and nations, and well as a belief in the subordination of the individual for the good of the state.

In that same paragraph, there is another reference that may elude some readers. Hill refers to standing at the graveside of John Barleycorn. John Barleycorn was a common term for whiskey and other alcoholic drinks and by "laying him away," Hill is referring to the ratification earlier that year of the 18th Amendment and the Volstead Act which would establish prohibition in the U.S. commencing the next month on January 16, 1920.

In Chapter 4, "When a Man Loves His Work" is reprinted from the October 1921 issue of *Napoleon Hill's Magazine*. In it, Hill predicts that President Harding would send in U.S. troops to settle the West Virginia mine wars. Hill's prediction was right. Harding did send in army troops, including an air squadron led by war hero Billy Mitchell. This confrontation was the culmination of a conflict that had gone on since the turn of the century between labor organizers and the mine owners who refused to allow their mines to become unionized. The ensuing conflict, known as the Battle of Blair Mountain, lasted about 5 days, and in the end those strikers who surrendered were sent home, while a number of the strike leaders were tried and jailed.

Although Blair Mountain did not end the labor problems that plagued the coalfields of West Virginia, the actions of President Harding brought things to a head and forced the owners and miners to seek less-volatile ways to resolve their differences.

In Chapter 5, "Initiative," reprinted from the August 1921 *Napoleon Hill's Magazine*, Hill makes reference to having taken a try at Thomas Edison's test questions. What he's referring to is a questionnaire created by Edison as a test for anyone who wanted to apply for a job as a manager of his company.

When *The New York Times* ran a story about the test, it became the talk of the town and everybody, including Napoleon Hill, was trying it out to see how well it would do. There were 150 questions covering everything from math and science to current events and personal habits. Applicants were given two hours to answer the questions, and most got a failing grade—including Edison's son Theodore, who was an MIT graduate in physics.

In Chapter 6, "Permanent Success," reprinted from the April 1921 *Napoleon Hill's Magazine*, Hill writes about Abraham Lincoln's humble birth and the hardships he endured growing up. In his comments, Hill mentions the name Nancy Hanks without explanation, knowing that his readers would immediately know who she was.

But times have changed, and what people learn in school or on their own through Google has changed even more, so it may be that the modern reader is not as well-versed in the finite details of history as was common in Hill's day. If that is so, you heard it here first: Nancy Hanks was Abe Lincoln's mother. She died October 5, 1818, when Abe was 9 years old. His father remarried a year later to Sarah Bush Johnson Lincoln.

The magazine stories and articles that make up the book are excerpted from issues of *Hill's Golden Rule* published between February 1919 and August 1920, and issues of *Napoleon Hill's Magazine* published between April 1921 and September 1923. Preceding each of the major stories is a reprint of the cover of the edition the item is taken from.

As you will have discovered by the time you come to the second story, these items do not follow one another in chronological order, but rather, have been arranged by subject in order to provide a comprehensive overview of Hill's philosophy.

As to the writing style and content, the intent of this book is to give you the chance to see what Napoleon Hill was like when he was first hitting his stride. We have opted to not update or modernize the stories and articles beyond offering the occasional editorial notes (set off in brackets) and to update some gendered references to be more inclusive. We have not converted Hill's references to money. However, if you would like to know what those amounts mean today, as a rule of thumb you can assume that $1,000 in 1920 would be comparable to approximately $13,600 today.

We close this introductory chapter with an item excerpted and adapted from the bestseller *Success Through a Positive Mental Attitude*, which was co-authored by Napoleon Hill with his friend and partner W. Clement Stone almost 40 years after the doors closed on Hill's magazines. It is called "How to Get the Most from Reading This Book," and some version of it appears in most publications from The Napoleon Hill Foundation.

HOW TO GET THE MOST FROM READING THIS BOOK

When you read, concentrate. Read as if the author were a close personal friend who is writing to you and you alone.

Spend a few minutes each day studying the principles and concepts contained in each article, in Napoleon Hill's own words.

Set aside a specific time each day, at least 15 minutes, to be spent reading and reflecting on how the things you have learned or the ideas you received can be applied in your own life. Choose a time when you are relaxed and your mind is receptive—and do it every day.

Take notes in the text, and jot down any flashes of inspiration, ideas, techniques, or answers to problems you discover while writing.

The R2/A2 Formula

Know what you are looking for as you read. Commit yourself to using the R2/A2 Formula: recognizing, relating, assimilating, and applying the principles, techniques, and ideas you read about in the book.

Your ability to use this formula will give you the key to open any door, meet any challenge, overcome any obstacle, and achieve wealth, happiness, and the true riches of life. Let's take a look at what the R2/A2 Formula looks like in practice:

- *Recognize*. Identify the principle, idea, or technique that is being used: "It helped someone else, I can see the results, and it will work for me if I use it."
- *Relate*. It is most important that you relate each concept to yourself and to your own actions and thoughts. Ask yourself, "What will the success principle, idea, or technique do for me?"
- *Assimilate*. Ask yourself, "How can I use this principle, idea, or technique to achieve my goals or solve my problems?"
- *Apply*. Ask yourself, "What actions will I take? When am I going to start?" Then follow through with the action.

Each ingredient in this formula is important. Each has special meaning and, when combined, will lead you to success. By using this formula, you will be able to focus your thinking to direct and guide you to achieve your objectives and your definitive goals in life.

Worthwhile Mental Exercises

After reading each article, ask yourself what ideas, principles, techniques, or formulas you discovered from it. How can you use each to adjust your behavior so it will become a part of you and help you to reach your personal objectives? What action will you take and when will you start?

CHAPTER TWO

The End of the Rainbow

"The End of the Rainbow" is a narrative of Hill's experience covering a period of more than twenty years. It shows how necessary it is to take into consideration events covering a long number of years in order to arrive at the vital truths of life. In all fiction, there has never been recorded a more dramatic scene than that which was actually experienced by the author of this narrative. The significance of "The Rainbow's End" lies not in any single event related, but in the interpretation of all the events and their relationship with one another.

PRELUDE

There is a legend, as old as the human race, which tells us that a pot of gold may be found at the end of a rainbow.

This fairy tale, which grips the imagination, may have something to do with the present tendency to worship at the shrine of Mammon.

For nearly fifteen years, I sought the end of my rainbow, that I might claim the pot of gold. My struggle in search of the evasive rainbow's end was ceaseless. It carried me up the mountainsides of failure and down the hillsides of despair, luring me on and on in search of the phantom pot of gold.

Lay aside your cares and come with me while I paint a picture of the winding pathway over which my search for the rainbow's end carried me. In this picture, I shall show you the seven important turning points of my life. Perhaps I can help you shorten the distance to your rainbow's end.

For the present, I will confine my narrative to the simple details of what I experienced in my search for the rainbow's end, as it carried me, time and time again, almost within reach of the coveted goal, then snatched it away from me.

As you retrace with me the footsteps of my pathway in search of the rainbow's end, you will see burrows of experience which have been plowed with thorns and watered with tears; you will walk with me down through the valley of the shadow; you will scale the mountain tops of expectation and find yourself suddenly crashing to the bottomless pits of despondency and failure; you will walk through green fields and crawl over sandy deserts.

Finally, we will arrive at the rainbow's end!

Be prepared for a shock, because you will see not only the pot of gold which legendary of the past has foretold, but you will find something else which is more to be coveted than all the gold on earth. Finding out what this "something" is shall be your reward for following me on this journey.

One morning, I was awakened abruptly, as if someone had shaken me. I looked around and found no one in the room. It was 3:00 A.M. In the fractional part of a minute, I saw a clear, concise picture which epitomized the seven turning points of my life, just as they are here described. I felt an impelling desire—it was much more than a desire; it was a command—to reduce the picture to words and use it as a public lecture.

Until this moment, I had failed, utterly, to correctly interpret many of my life's experiences, some of which had left scars of disappointment on my heart and a touch of bitterness which somewhat colored and modified my efforts to be a constructive servant of the people.

You will pardon me if I refrain from trying to express my real feelings during this moment when the last lingering touch of intolerance was wiped out of my heart, and I saw, for the first time in my life, the real significance of those trying experiences, those heartaches, those disappointments, and those hardships which overtake all of us at one time or another. I ask that you pardon me for omitting the description of my real feelings on this occasion, not alone because of the sacredness of the experience, but because of lack of words with which to correctly interpret my feelings.

With this foundation, you may come with me to the beginning of the first important turning point in my life, which happened more than twenty years ago, while I was a homeless lad without education and without an aim in life. I was floating helplessly on the sea of life as a dry leaf would float on the bosom of the winds. As well as I can remember, no ambition higher than that of being a laborer in the coal mines had ever reached my mind. The hand of fate seemed to be against me. I believed in no one except God and myself, and sometimes I wondered if God were not double crossing me.

I was cynical and filled with skepticism and doubt. I believed in nothing I couldn't understand. Two and two meant four to me only when I put down the figures and had done the adding myself. All of which, I freely admit, is a prosaic, uneventful beginning for this narrative, a fact for which I am in no way responsible since I am here setting down only that which happened. And, may it not be well if I here digress just a moment while I remind you that most early life experiences are uneventful, dry, and prosaic. This point seems so vital that I feel impelled to turn the spotlight on it before I proceed with my narrative, that it may become an illuminating factor in helping you to interpret the experiences of your own life in the light of the real significance of every event, no matter how insignificant it may have seemed at the time. I am convinced that too often, we look for the important events in life to come in a dramatic, impressive, and staged manner, whereas in reality, they come and go unnoticed except for the joy and grief which they bring, and we lose sight of the real lessons they teach while we fix our attention upon this joy or grief.

FIRST TURNING POINT

I was sitting before the fire one night, discussing with older people the question of unrest upon the part of laboring men. The labor union movement had just commenced to make itself felt in that part of the country where I then lived, and the tactics used by the organizers impressed me as being too revolutionary and destructive to ever bring permanent success to the laboring people.

I felt very deeply on this subject and expressed my feelings accordingly, reasoning along the line that there were two sides to the question, and that both the employers and the employees were guilty, to some extent, of tactics which were highly destructive and led not to cooperation, but to misunderstanding and disagreement.

One of the men who sat before that fireside with me made a remark which proved to be the first important turning point in my life. He reached over and firmly grasped me by the shoulder, looked me squarely in the eyes, and said:

"Why, you are a bright boy, and if you would give yourself an education, you would make your mark in the world."

The first concrete result of that remark caused me to enroll for a course in a business college, a step which I am duty-bound bound to admit proved to be one of the most helpful I ever took, because I got my first fleeting glimpse, in my business college training, of what one might call a fair sense of proportions. Here I learned the spirit of simple democracy, and most important of all, I got a hold of the idea that it would pay me to perform more service and better service than I was actually paid to perform. This idea has become a fixed principle with me, and it now modifies all of my actions wherein I render service.

/ ENTREPRENEUR TIP

How can your business serve its community beyond providing goods or services? The answer could be social entrepreneurship. By including a social justice element to your business through volunteerism, donations, or selling products/services with a social impact, you can still realize profits while leading the charge for greater socioeconomic parity in your community.

In business college, I rubbed elbows with young men and young women who, like myself, were there for only one purpose, and that was to learn to render efficient service and earn a living. I met people from many traditions and backgrounds all on exactly the same terms, and learned for the first time that all were human and all responded to that simple spirit of democracy which prevailed in the business college environment.

After finishing my business college training, I secured a position as a stenographer and bookkeeper and worked in this capacity for the ensuing five years. As a result of this idea of performing more service and better service than paid for, which I had learned in business college, I advanced rapidly and always succeeded in filling positions of responsibility far in advance of my years, with salary proportionate.

I saved money and soon had a bank account amounting to several thousand dollars. I was rapidly advancing toward my rainbow's end. I aimed to succeed, and my idea of success was the same as that which dominates the average youth's mind today, namely, money. I saw my bank account growing bigger and bigger. I saw myself advancing in position and earning more and more salary. My method of rendering service that was greater in quality and quantity than that for which I was paid was so unusual that it attracted attention, and I profited by contrast with those who had not learned that secret.

My reputation spread rapidly, and I found competitive bidders for my services. I was in demand, not because of what I knew, which was little enough, but because of my willingness to make the best use of what little I did know. This spirit of willingness proved to be the most powerful and strategic principle ever learned.

> ### *ɪ* ENTREPRENEUR TIP
> Expand your skill set with that spirit of willingness in mind. One way to do that is to step up in your local service organizations or professional associations to serve on committees, lead initiatives, and network just a bit outside of your comfort zone.

SECOND TURNING POINT

The tides of fate blew me southward, and I became the sales manager for a large lumber manufacturing company. I knew nothing about lumber, and I knew nothing about sales management, but I had learned that it paid to render better service and more of it than I was paid for, and with this principle as the dominating spirit, I tackled my new job with the determination to find out all I could about selling lumber.

I was a good employee. My salary was increased twice during the year, and my bank account was growing bigger and bigger. I did so well in managing the sales of my employer's lumber that he organized a new lumber company and took me into partnership with him, as a half owner in the business.

The lumber business was good, and we prospered.

I could see myself drawing nearer and nearer to the rainbow's end. Money and success poured in on me from every direction, all of which fixed my attention steadfastly on the pot of gold which I could plainly see just ahead of me. Up to this time, it had never occurred to me that success could consist of anything except gold. Money in the bank represented the last word in attainment. Being of that breezy, good-fellow type, I made friends rapidly in the lumber circles and soon developed into a front-row man at the lumber conventions and at gatherings of lumbermen.

I was succeeding rapidly, and I knew it.

Above everything else, I knew I was engaged in exactly the business for which I was best suited. Nothing could have induced me to change my business—that is, nothing except that which happened.

I strutted around under the influence of my vanity until I had commended to feel my importance. In the light of more sober years and more accurate interpretation of human events, I now wonder if an unseen hand does not purposely permit us foolish human beings to parade before our own mirror of vanity until we come to see how vulgar we are acting and quit it. At any rate, I seemed to have a clear track ahead, there was coal in the bunker, water in the tank, my hand was on the throttle, and I opened it wide.

Fate was awaiting me just around the bend, with a stuffed club, and it was not stuffed with cotton, but of course I did not see the impending crash until it came. Mine was a sad story, but not unlike that which many another might tell if they would be frank with themselves.

Like a stroke of lightning out of a clear sky, the 1907 panic swept down on me. Overnight, it swept away every dollar I had. The person with whom I was in business withdrew, panic stricken, but without loss, and left me with nothing but the empty shell of a company that owned nothing except a good reputation. I could have bought a hundred thousand dollars' worth of lumber on that reputation. A crooked lawyer (who afterward served a term in the penitentiary for some other offense, the details of which are too numerous to be enumerated) saw a chance to cash the reputation and what was left of the lumber company that had been left on my hands. He and a group of other men purchased the company and continued to operate it. I learned a year later that they bought every dollar's worth of lumber that they could get hold of, resold it, and pocketed the proceeds without paying for it; thus, I had been the innocent means of helping them defraud their creditors who learned after it was too late that I was in no way connected with the company.

That failure, while it worked a hardship on those who suffered loss as a result of my reputation having been wrongly used, proved to be the second important turning point in my life, because it forced me out of a business which offered no possibility of any remuneration except money, and no opportunity for personal growth from "within." I fought with all my might and main to save my company during the panic, but I was as helpless as a suckling babe, and the swirl carried me, like a dry leaf on the winds, out of the lumber business and into a law school where I succeeded in rubbing off some more of my ignorance, vanity, and illiteracy, a trio against which no person can successfully compete.

I ENTREPRENEUR TIP

When you have to pivot due to outside circumstances, do you freeze in your tracks, or use it as the opportunity to rethink your processes? Sudden shifts in your work routine open up the chance to effect change on the fly, allowing you to meet the moment with enhanced creativity. The next time the wind shifts suddenly in your business, use the time as a chance to pivot unapologetically.

THIRD TURNING POINT

It required the 1907 panic and the failure which it brought me to divert and redirect my efforts from the lumber business to the study of law. Nothing on earth except failure, or what I then called failure, could have brought about this result; thus, the second important turning point of my life was ushered in on the wings of failure, which reminds me to state that there is a great lesson in every failure whether we learn what it is or not.

When I entered law school, it was with the firm belief that I would emerge doubly prepared to catch up with the end of the rainbow and claim my pot of gold. I still had no higher aspiration than that of accumulating money; yet, the very thing which I worshipped most seemed to be the most elusive thing on earth, for it was always evading me, always in sight, but always just out of reach.

I attended law school at night and worked as an automobile salesman during the day. My sales experience in the lumber business was turned to good advantage. I prospered rapidly, doing so well that (still featuring the habit of performing more service and better service than paid for) the opportunity came to enter the automobile manufacturing business. I saw the need for automobile mechanics; therefore, I opened an educational department and began to train ordinary machinists in automobile assembling and repair work. This school prospered until it was paying me over a thousand dollars a month in net profits.

Again, I saw my rainbow's end in sight. Again, I knew I had at last found my niche in the world's work. Again, I knew that nothing could swerve me from my course or cause me to divert my attention from the automobile business. My banker saw me prospering. He extended me credit for expansion. He encouraged me to invest in outside lines of business. My banker was one of the finest people in the world, so he appeared to me. He loaned me many thousands of dollars on my own signature, without endorsement.

But, alas, it were ever thus—the sweet usually precedes the bitter.

My banker loaned me money until I was hopelessly in debt; then he took over my business. It all happened so suddenly that it dazed me. I didn't think such a thing possible. You see, I had still to learn much about the ways of men, especially the type of men which, unfortunately, my banker turned out to be, a type which, in justice to the business of banking, I ought to say is rarely found in that business.

From a man of affairs, with a net income of over a thousand dollars a month, owner of half a dozen automobiles and much other junk which I didn't need but didn't know it, I was suddenly reduced to poverty.

The rainbow's end disappeared, and it was many years afterward before I learned that this failure was probably the greatest single blessing that ever was showered upon me, because it forced me out of a business which in no way helped to develop the human side, and diverted my efforts into a channel which brought me a rich experience which I greatly needed.

I believe it worthy of note to here state that I went back to Washington, D.C. a few years after this event and, out of curiosity, visited the old bank where I once had a liberal line of credit, expecting, of course, to find a prosperous bank still in operation.

To my great dismay, I found that the bank had gone out of business, and the banking house was being used as a lunchroom, and my erstwhile banker friend had been reduced to penury and want. I met him on the streets, practically penniless. With eyes red and swollen, he aroused in me a questioning attitude, and I wondered, for the first time in my life, if one might find any other thing of value, except money, at the rainbow's end.

But, mind you, this temporary questioning attitude was not an open rebellion by any means, nor did I pursue it far enough to get the answer. It merely came as a fleeting thought, and passed out of my mind. Had I known as much then about interpreting human events as I now know, I would have recognized that circumstance was a gentle nudge which the unseen hand was giving me. Had I known anything about the law of compensation, I would not have been surprised when I found my banker friend reduced to poverty, knowing as I did, after it was too late, that my experience was but one of hundreds of similar ones which marked his code of business ethics.

I never put up a stronger battle in my life than I did in trying to remain in the automobile business. I borrowed $4,000 from my wife and sunk it in a vain effort to remain in what I believed to be the business for which I was best fitted. But forces over which I had no control, and which I did not understand at that time, would have none of my efforts to remain in the automobile business. It was at a heavy cost of pride that I finally submitted and turned, for want of knowing what else to do, to using the knowledge of law which I had acquired.

I ENTREPRENEUR TIP

Failure happens every day. And that's a good thing! Take five minutes to jot down the ebbs and flows you have noticed in your entrepreneurial journey, or even in your day-to-day business activities. How do those ebbs and flows affect your productivity, the habits you create, and the goals you set?

FOURTH TURNING POINT

Because I was my wife's husband, and her people had influence, I secured the appointment as assistant to the chief counsel for one of the largest corporations of its kind in the world. My salary was greatly out of proportion to those which the company had usually paid beginners, and still further out of proportion to what I was worth, but pull was pull, and I was there because I was there. It turned out that what I lacked in legal ability, I supplied through that one sound fundamental principle which I had learned in business collegially, namely, to render more service and better service than paid for, wherever possible.

I was holding my position without difficulty. I practically had a berth for life if I cared to keep it. One day, I did what my close personal friends and relatives said was a very foolish thing. I quit my job abruptly. When pressed for a reason, I gave what seemed to me to be a very sound one, but I had trouble convincing the family circle that I had acted wisely, and still greater difficulty in convincing a few of my friends that I was perfectly rational in mind.

I quit that position because I found the work too easy, and I was performing it with too little effort. I saw myself drifting into the habit of inertia. I felt myself loving to take things easily. There was no particular impelling urge that forced or induced me to keep moving. I was among friends and relatives. I had a job that I could keep as long as I wished it, at a salary that provided a home, a good car, and enough gasoline to run it.

What else did I need? This was the attitude toward which I felt myself slipping. It was an attitude that startled me. However ignorant I might have been in other matters at that time, I have always felt thankful for having had enough sense to realize that strength and growth come only from struggle, that disuse brings atrophy and decay.

This move proved to be the next most important turning point in my life, although it was followed by ten years of effort which brought almost every grief that the human heart could experience. I quit my job in the legal field, where I was getting along well, living among friends and relatives, with what I believed to be a bright and unusually promising future ahead of me. I am frank to admit that it has always been a source of wonderment to me as to why and how I gathered the courage to make the move that I did. As far as I am able to correctly interpret, I arrived at my decision more in the nature of a "hunch," or as a prompting which I little understood, than I did by logical deduction.

I selected Chicago as a location because I believed it to be the most competitive field in the world, feeling, as I did, that if I could come to Chicago and gain recognition along any legitimate line, I would prove to myself that I had material in me that might someday develop into real ability. That was a queer process of reasoning; at least it was an unusual process for me at that time, which reminds me to admit that we human beings often take unto ourselves credit or intelligence to which we are not entitled. I fear that we too often assume credit for wisdom and for results which accrue from causes over which we have absolutely no control, and for which we are in no way responsible.

This is a thought which, I am duty-bound to state, runs like a golden cord throughout my analysis of the seven most important turning points of my life. While I do not mean to convey the impression that all of our acts are controlled by causes beyond our power to direct, I strongly urge upon you the wisdom of studying and correctly interpreting those causes which mark the vital turning points in our lives, the points at which our efforts are diverted from one direction to another, in spite of all we can do. I offer you no theory or hypothesis to cover this strange anomaly, believing that you will find your answer through the interpretative power of your religion, whatever it may be.

I came to Chicago without so much as a letter of introduction. My aim was to sell myself on merit, or at least on what I suspected of being merit. I secured a position as advertising manager. I knew next to nothing about advertising, but my previous experience as a salesman came to my rescue, and my old friend, the habit of performing more service than paid for, gave me a fair balance on the credit side of the ledger.

The first year I earned $5,200!

I was "coming back" by leaps and bounds. Gradually, the rainbow began to circle around me, and I saw, once more, the shining pot of gold almost within my reach. I believe it of significant importance to bear in mind the fact that my standard of success was always measured in terms of dollars, and my rainbow's end promised nothing but a pot of gold. Up to this point, if the thought ever entered my mind that anything except a pot of gold might be found at the end of a rainbow, that thought was momentary and left but a slight impression behind it.

All back down the ages, history is full of evidence that a feast usually precedes a fall. I was having my feast but did not expect a fall to follow it. I suspect that no one ever does anticipate the fall until it comes, but come it will, unless one's fundamental guiding principles are sound.

FIFTH TURNING POINT

I did well as advertising manager. The president of the company was attracted by my work and later helped organize the Betsy Ross Candy Company, and I became its president, thus beginning the next most important turning point of my life.

The business began to expand until we had a chain of stores in 18 different cities. Again, I saw my rainbow's end almost within reach. I knew that I had at last found the business in which I wanted to remain for life, yet when I frankly admit that our policy and our business was fashioned after that of another candy company, whose Western manager was my personal friend and former business associate, and that his overwhelmingly large success was the main factor in causing me to enter the candy business, you will be able to anticipate the finish of our candy enterprise before I mention it. Pardon me for digressing for a moment while I philosophize on a point which has brought deserved defeat to millions of people—namely, the practice of appropriating another person's plan instead of working out a plan of one's own origin. The public is never in sympathy with the trailer who is obviously copying someone else's plan, even though such practice is not prohibited legally.

/ ENTREPRENEUR TIP

Be mindful when gauging the perspective of outside groups—or those within your organization who have decision-making power. Want to be a part of a group without giving in to groupthink? Create a coalition of people in your industry and find a time each month to meet up and discuss common concerns and issues that affect your business. By reaching out to colleagues outside of your own business, you can talk about those issues without the concern of inter-office politics affecting the conversations.

Nor is the resentment of the public the most damaging factor with which one who makes this mistake must contend; the practice seems to take away the enthusiasm which a person usually puts into a plan which is conceived in his own heart and brought to maturity in his own brain.

Everything went smoothly for a time, until my business associate and a third man, whom we later took into the business, took a notion to gain control of my interest without paying for it, a mistake which people never seem to understand they are making until it is too late and they have paid the price of their folly.

Their plan worked, but I balked more stiffly than they had anticipated; therefore, to gently urge me along toward the "grand exit," they had me arrested on a false charge and offered to settle out of court if I would turn over my interest in the company. I refused and insisted on going to trial on the charge. When the time arrived, no one was present to prosecute. We insisted on prosecution and requested the court to summon the complaining witness and make him prosecute, which was done.

The judge, Honorable Arnold Heap, stopped the proceedings and threw the case out of court before it had gone very far, with the statement that, "This is one of the most flagrant cases of attempted coercion that has ever come before me."

To protect my character, I brought suit for $50,000 damages. The case was tried five years later, and I secured a heavy judgment in the superior court of Chicago. The suit was what is called a "tort action," meaning that it claimed damages for malicious injury to reputation. A judgment secured under a tort action carries with it the right to imprison the one against whom the judgment is secured until the judgment is paid.

But, I suspect that another and much more exacting law than that under which tort actions may be brought was operating during those five years, because one of the parties—the one in whose brain the plan to have me arrested as a part to their plan to coerce my interest in the business away from me—was serving a term in the federal penitentiary before my action against him was tried, and for a crime separate and apart from the one he had committed against me. The other party had fallen from a high station in life to poverty and disgrace.

My judgment stands on the records of the superior court of Chicago as silent evidence of vindication of my character and as evidence of something far more important than mere vindication of character, namely, that the unseen hand which guides the destiny of all who earnestly seek truth had eliminated from my nature all desire for my "pound of flesh." My judgment against my traducers was not collected and it never will be. At least I will never collect it, because I suspect that it has been paid, many times over, in blood and remorse and regret and failure visited upon those who would have destroyed my character for personal gain.

This was one of the greatest single blessings that ever came to me, because it taught me to forgive; it taught me, also, that the law of compensation is always and everywhere in operation, and that "whatsoever a person soweth, that shall they also reap." It blotted out of my nature the last lingering thought of seeking personal revenge, at any time, under any circumstances. It taught me that time is the friend of all who are right and the mortal enemy of all who are unjust and destructive in their efforts.

Once, I took out my watch, it slipped from my hands and crashed to pieces on the floor. I picked up the dead remains of what was a splendid time piece only a few moments ago, and as I turned it over and looked at it, I was reminded that nothing ever "just happens." That my watch was created by a superior, to perform a definite work, according to a definite plan. How much more certain it is that we human beings were created by a superior, according to a definite plan, to perform a definite work.

What a blessing it is when we come into realization of the fact that probably we were not intended as destructive factors, and that everything which we accumulate in the way of material wealth will finally become as useless as the dust to which our flesh and bones will return.

I sometimes wonder if a full realization of this truth does not come more easily to the person who has been sinned against and spat upon and slandered and crucified on the cross of ignorance. I sometimes wonder if it were not well for all of us to undergo these experiences which try our faith and exhaust our patience and cause us to lose control of ourselves and strike back, because we learn, in this way, the futility of hatred and envy and selfishness and the tendency to destroy or undermine the happiness of a fellow being.

We can sharpen our intellect through the experiences of others, but our emotions are vitalized and developed only through our own personal experiences; therefore, we can profit by every experience which works upon our emotions, whether that experience brings joy or grief. A close search of the biographies of people of destiny discloses the fact that nearly every one of them was sorely tried in the mill of merciless experience before they arrived, which leads me to wonder if the unseen hand does not test the mettle of the person in various and sundry ways before placing serious responsibilities upon their shoulders.

SIXTH TURNING POINT

We come now to the turning point which probably brought me nearer the rainbow's end than any of the others had, because it placed me in a position where I found it necessary to bring into use all the knowledge that I had acquired up to that time concerning every subject with which I was familiar, and gave me opportunity for self-expression and for personal development such as rarely comes to a person early in life. This turning point came when, after having been forced out of the candy business, I turned my efforts toward teaching advertising and sales.

Some wise philosopher has said that we never learn much until we commence trying to teach others. My experience as a teacher proved that this is true. My school prospered from the start. I had a resident school and a correspondence school through which I was teaching students in nearly every English-speaking country.

In spite of the ravages of war, my school was growing by leaps and bounds, and I saw the end of my rainbow drawing nearer and nearer. I was so close to it that I could almost reach out and touch the pot of gold. As a result of the record which I was making and the recognition I was gaining, I attracted the attention of the head of a corporation who employed me for three weeks out of each month at a salary of $150,200 a year, considerably more than the President of the United States receives.

In less than six months, largely as a result of a series of strokes of good luck, I built up one of the most efficient working forces in America, and increased the assets of the company to where it was offered $20 million dollars more for its business than it was worth when I took hold of its affairs.

Candidly, had you been in my place, would you not have felt justified in saying that you had found your rainbow's end? Would you not have felt justified in saying that you had attained success?

I thought I had, but I had one of the rudest shocks of all awaiting me, due partly to the dishonesty of the head of the corporation for whom I was working, but more directly, I suspect, to a deeper and more significant cause concerning that which fate seemed to have decreed that I should learn something. $100,000 of my salary was conditional upon my remaining as the directing head of the staff for a period of one year. In less than half that time, I began to see that I was pyramiding power and placing it in the hands of a person who was growing drunk on it. I began to see that ruin awaited him just around the corner. This discovery brought me much grief. Morally, I was responsible for several million dollars of capital which I had induced the American people to invest in this corporation. Legally, of course, I was in no way responsible.

I finally brought the matter to a head, delivering an ultimatum to the head of the corporation to safeguard the funds of the company under a board of financial control or else accept my resignation. He laughed at the suggestion, because he thought I would not break my contract and thereby lose $100,000. Perhaps I would not have done so had it not been for the moral responsibility which I felt obliged to carry out in behalf of thousands of investors. I resigned, had the company placed in the hands of the receiver, and thereby protected it against the mismanagement of a money-mad young man, a bit of satisfaction which brought me much ridicule from my friends and cost me $100,000.

For the moment, my rainbow's end seemed vague and somewhat distant.

There were moments when I wondered what caused me to make a fool of myself and throw away a fortune just to protect those who never would even know that I had made a sacrifice for them.

It was during one of these reminiscent moments that I felt a bell ringing in the region of my heart. At least the ringing of a bell is as near as I can come to describing the sensation which I experienced. With the ringing of this bell came a message—a clear, distinct, unmistakable message. It bade me stand by my decision and be thankful that I had the courage to render it as I did. Remember what I have said about this ringing bell, because I am coming back to the subject again. Since that eventful moment, I have felt the ringing of the bell many times. I have now come to understand what it means. I respond to it, and the message which follows it guides me in the right direction. Perhaps you would not have called the sensation which I experienced the ringing of the bell a message, but I know of no other terms in which to describe these, the strangest of my life's experiences.

At this point, I commenced to experience something more than the ringing of a bell. I commenced to wonder if my rainbow's end had not been evading me all these years, leading me up one hillside of failure and down another, because I was looking for the wrong reward. Mind you, I just questioned myself on this point, that was all.

This brings me to the seventh and last important turning point in my life.

Before I proceed to describe this last turning point, I feel it my duty to say that nothing which has been described up to this point is, within itself, of any practical significance. The six turning points which I have described, taken singly, meant absolutely nothing to me, and will mean nothing to you if they are analyzed separately. But, take these events collectively, and they form a foundation for the next and last turning point, and constitute the very best sort of evidence that we human beings are constantly undergoing evolutionary changes as a result of the varying experiences with which we meet, even though no single experience seems to convey a definite, usable lesson.

I feel impelled to dwell at length on the point which I am here trying to make plain, because I am now at that point in my career at which people go down in defeat or rise to heights of attainment which startle the world, according to the manner in which they interpret past events and build plans that are based upon past experiences. If my story stopped where I am at this moment, it could not possibly mean anything to you, but there is another and more significant chapter yet to be written covering the seventh and last important turning point in my life.

Up to the present point, I have presented nothing but a more or less disconnected series of events which, within themselves, mean nothing. I repeat this thought because I want you to get it. And, while you are thinking about it, I want to remind you that it is necessary to take a retrospective view of life every so often with the object of gathering all the more or less meaningless events together and interpreting them in the light of trying to discover what has been learned from them.

These experiences and failures and disappointments and mistakes and turning points in life might go on and on without benefiting until the grim reaper arrives and claims his toll unless we awake to the realization that there are lessons to be learned from every one of them, and unless we commence tabulating the results of what we learn from those experiences so we can make use of them without having to repeat them over and over.

SEVENTH TURNING POINT

In my climax, I will tabulate the sum total of all that I learned from each of the seven important mileposts of my life, but first let me describe the seventh and last of these turning points. To do so, I must go back one year to that eventful day, November 11, 1918.

That was Armistice Day (now known as Veterans Day), as everyone knows. Like most other people, I became as drunk with enthusiasm and joy that day as any person ever did on wine. I was practically penniless, but I was happy to know that the slaughter was over, and reason was about to spread its beneficent wings over the earth once more.

The war had swept away my school, from which my income would have amounted to over $15,000 a year had our boys not been drafted for war, and I stood as far away from my rainbow's end as I did on that eventful day more than twenty years previously, when I stood at the drift mouth of a coal mine where I was employed as a laborer and thought of that statement which a kindly old gentleman had made to me the night before, but realized that a yawning chasm stood between me and any accomplishment other than that of laborer in the mines.

But I was happy again. Again, that thought entered my consciousness and prompted me to ask myself if I had not been searching for the wrong sort of reward at my rainbow's end.

I sat down to my typewriter with nothing particular in mind. To my astonishment, my hands began to play a regular symphony upon the keys of the typewriter. I had never written so rapidly or so easily before. I did not think of what I was writing. I just wrote and wrote and kept on writing.

When I was through, I had five pages of manuscript, and as near as I have been able to determine, that manuscript was written without any organized thought on my part. It was an editorial out of which my first magazine, *Hill's Golden Rule*, was born. I took this editorial to a wealthy man and read it to him. Before I had read the last line, he had promised to finance my magazine.

It was in this somewhat dramatic manner that a desire which had lain dormant in my mind for nearly twenty years began to express itself in reality. It was the same idea which I had in mind when I made the statement which caused that old gentleman to lay his hand on my shoulder and make that fortunate remark, twenty years previously, which had as its foundation the thought that the Golden Rule ought to be the guiding spirit in all human relationships.

All my life, I had wanted to become a newspaper editor. Back more than thirty years ago, when I was a very small boy, I used to "kick" the press for my father who published a small newspaper, and I grew to love the smell of printer's ink.

Perhaps this desire was subconsciously gaining momentum until it finally had to burst forth in terms of action; or maybe there was another plan over which I had no control, and with the building of which I had nothing to do, that urged me on and on, never giving me a moment's rest in any other line of work until I began my first magazine. The point can be passed for the moment.

The important thing to which I would direct your attention is the fact that I found my proper niche in the world's work, and I was very happy over it. Strange enough, I entered upon this work, which constituted my last lap in the long, long trail over which I had traveled in search of my rainbow's end, with never a thought of finding a pot of gold. For the first time in my life, I seemed to sense the fact that there was something else to be sought in life that was worth more than gold; therefore, I went at my first editorial work with only one thought in mind—and I pause while you ponder over this thought—and that thought was to render the world the best service of which I was capable.

The magazine prospered from the beginning. In less than six months, it was being read in every English-speaking country in the world. It had brought me recognition from all parts of the world, which resulted in a public speaking tour which I made in 1920, covering every large city in America. This tour was a whole education within itself because it brought me in exceedingly close touch with the people in all walks of life, in all parts of the country, and gave me an opportunity to study their needs, their desires, and their emotions.

Up to and including the sixth of the important turning points in my life, I had made about as many enemies as I had friends. Now a strange thing has happened. Beginning with my first editorial work, I commenced to make friends by the thousands; until today, upwards of 100,000 people stand squarely back of me because they believe in me and my message.

What brought about this change?

If you understand the law of attraction, you can answer this, because you know that like attracts like, and that a person will attract friends or foes, according to the nature of the thoughts which dominate their mind. One cannot take a belligerent attitude toward life and expect others to take anything except the same attitude toward him. When I commenced to preach the Golden Rule in my first magazine, I commenced to live it as near as I could. There is a big difference between merely believing in the Golden Rule and actually practicing it in overt acts, a truth which I learned when I began my first magazine. This realization brought me abruptly into understanding of a principle which now permeates every thought that finds a permanent lodging place in my mind, and dominates every act I perform, as nearly as is humanly possible, and that thought is none other than the one laid down by the Master in his sermon on the mount when he admonished us to do unto others as we would have others do unto us.

During these past three years, since I have been sending out Golden Rule thoughts to hundreds of thousands of people, these thought waves have multiplied themselves in the rebound and have brought back to me floods of goodwill from those whom my message reached. "Whatsoever a person soweth, that shall they also reap." I have been sowing seeds of kindness; I have been planting constructive thoughts where destructive ones existed before; I have been helping people see the folly of fighting among themselves and the virtue of cooperative effort, until I have charged and vitalized my very soul with these as my dominating thoughts, and they, in turn, have constituted a magnet which has attracted back to me the cooperation and good will of thousands who were in harmony with these thoughts.

I was rapidly approaching my rainbow's end for the seventh and last time. Every avenue of failure seemed closed. My enemies had been slowly transformed into friends, and I was making new friends by the thousand. But, there was a final test which I had to undergo.

The unseen hand does not hand over its precious jewels of knowledge without a price, nor does it lift people into positions of responsibility or create people of destiny without testing their mettle. This testing process usually takes place when people least expect it, thereby catching them off guard and giving them no chance to display anything except their real personalities. When my testing time arrived, it caught me unexpectedly and unprepared, due mainly, I suppose, to the fact that I had protected my flanks with nothing more than man-made appliances. I had relied too much on myself and not enough on the unseen hand. I had failed to strike a happy medium at which I maintained just enough, but not too much self-reliance; consequently, my last and most trying turning point brought me much grief which I could have avoided had my knowledge of human events and of that power which controls human events been a little better balanced.

As I have stated, I was approaching the end of my rainbow with the firm belief that nothing on earth could stop me from attaining it and claiming my pot of old and everything else that a successful searcher for this great reward might expect.

Like a stroke of lightning out of a clear sky, I received a shock.

The "impossible" had happened. My first magazine, *Hill's Golden Rule*, was not only snatched out of my hands overnight, but its influence which I had built up was temporarily turned as a weapon to defeat me.

Again, my fellow humans had failed me. And I thought unkind thoughts about them. It was a blow to me when I awoke to the realization that there was no truth to the Golden Rule which I had been not only preaching to thousands of people, through the pages of my magazine, and in person to hundreds of thousands, but had been doing my level best to live as well.

This was the supreme moment of test.

Had my experience proved my most beloved principles to be false and nothing more than a snare with which to trip the untutored, or was I about to learn a great lesson which would establish the truth and the soundness of those principles for the remainder of my natural life and perhaps throughout eternity?

These are the questions which passed through my mind.

I did not answer them quickly. I could not. I was so stunned that I simply had to stop and catch my breath. I had been preaching that one could not steal another person's idea or his plans or his goods and wares and still prosper. My experience seemed to give the lie to all I had ever written or spoken along this line, because the men who stole the child of my heart and brain seemed not only to be prospering with it, but they had actually used it as a means of stopping me from carrying out my plans for worldwide service in the interest of the human race.

Months passed by, and I was unable to turn a wheel.

I had been deposed, my magazine had been taken away from me, and my friends seemed to look upon me as a sort of fallen hero. Some said I would come back stronger and bigger for the experience. Others said I was through. Thus, the remarks came and went, but I stood looking on in wonderment, feeling much the same as a person feels who is undergoing a nightmare and knows what is going on around him but is unable to awake or move as much as a little finger.

Literally, I was experiencing a wide-awake nightmare which seemed to hold me firmly within its grasp. My courage was gone. My faith in humanity was all but gone. My love for humanity was weakening. Slowly but surely, I was reversing my opinion concerning the highest and best ideals which I had been building for more than a score of years. The passing weeks seemed like an eternity. The days seemed like a whole lifetime.

But one day, the atmosphere began to clear away.

And, I am reminded to digress while I say that such atmospheres usually do clear way. Time is a wonderful healer of wounds. Time cures nearly everything that is sick or ignorant, and most of us are both at times.

During the seventh and last turning point in my life, I was reduced to greater poverty than any I had ever known before. From a well-furnished home, I was reduced, practically overnight, to a one-room apartment. Coming, as this blow did, just as I was about to lay hold of the pot of gold at my rainbow's end, it cut a deep and ugly wound in my heart. During this brief testing spell, I was made to kneel in the very dust of poverty and eat the crusts of all my past follies. When I had all but given up, the clouds of darkness began to float away as rapidly as they had covered me.

I stood face-to-face with one of the most trying tests that every came to me. Perhaps no human being was more severely tried than I was. At least that was the way I felt about it at the time.

The postman had delivered my scant collection of mail. As I opened it, I was watching the pale red sun as it had all but disappeared over the western horizon. To me, it was symbolic of that which was about to happen to me, for I saw my sun of hope also setting in the West.

I slit open the envelope on top, and as I did so, a Certificate of Deposit fluttered to the floor and fell face upward. It was for $25,000. For a whole minute, I stood with my eyes glued to that bit of paper, wondering if I were not dreaming. I walked over closer to it, picked it up, and read the letter which accompanied it.

That money was all mine! I could draw it out of the bank at will. Only two slight strings were tied to it, but those strings made it necessary for me to obligate myself, morally, to turn my back on everything that I had been preaching about placing the interests of the people above those of any individual.

The supreme moment of test had come.

Would I accept that money, which was ample capital with which to publish my magazine, or would I return it and carry on a little longer? Those were the first questions which claimed my attention.

Then I heard the ringing of the bell in the region of my heart. This time, its sound was more direct. It caused the blood to tingle through my body. With the ringing of the bell came the most direct command that ever registered itself in my consciousness, and that command was accompanied by a chemical change in my brain such as I had never experienced before. It was a positive, startling command, and it brought a message which I could not misunderstand.

Without promise of reward, it bade me return that $25,000.

I hesitated. The bell kept on ringing. My feet seemed glued to the spot. I could not move out of my tracks. Then I reached my decision. I decided to heed that prompting, which no one but a fool could have mistaken.

The instant I reached this conclusion, I looked, and in the approaching twilight, I saw the rainbow's end. I had at last caught up with it. I saw no pot of gold, except the one which I was about to send back to the source from which it came, but I found something more precious than all the gold in the world as I heard a voice which reached me not through my ears, but through my heart, and it said:

"Standeth God Within the Shadows of Every Failure."

The end of my rainbow brought me the triumph of principle over gold. It gave me a closer communion with the great unseen forces of this universe, and new determination to plant the seed of the Golden Rule philosophy in the hearts of millions of other weary travelers who are seeking the end of their rainbow.

Did it pay to return that $25,000?

Well, I leave that to my readers to decide. Personally, I am well satisfied with my decision, following which a strange and unexpected thing happened—all the capital I needed came not from one source alone, but from many sources. It came in abundance, without any chain of gold tied to it or any embarrassing conditions placed upon it which sought to control my pen.

In the July issue of this magazine, my secretary tells of one of the most dramatic events which followed closely upon my decision not to accept financial help from sources that would, to any extent whatsoever, control my pen. That incident is only one, each constituting sufficient evidence to convince all but fools that the Golden Rule really works, the law of compensation is still in operation, and, "Whatsoever a person soweth, that shall they also reap."

Not alone did I get all the capital necessary to carry this magazine over the beginning period, during which its own revenues were insufficient to publish it, but what is of far greater significant, the magazine is growing with rapidity heretofore unknown in the field of similar periodicals. The readers and the public generally have caught the spirit back of the work we are doing, and they have put the law of increasing returns into operation in our favor.

Am I entitled to any credit for the events herein mentioned, some of which would seem to reflect credit upon me? Am I entitled to credit for the success which is now crowning the efforts I am exerting through the pages of this magazine?

Frankly, I feel impelled to answer in the negative.

I have been nothing more than a tool in the hands of a higher power, and I have played about the same part which a violin plays in the hands of a master. If I have struck a symphonic rhythm in the song I am trying to sing through the pages of this, the people's monthly messenger, it has been because I have resigned myself to the influence of the unseen hand. What I am trying to say is that I take no credit unto myself for anything of a creditable nature which I have done or may do. Had I followed what seemed to be my natural tendency and inclinations, I would have gone down to defeat at any one of the seven turning points in my life, but always there was a guiding force which came to my rescue and saved me from defeat.

I make these admissions in a spirit of frankness and with the earnest desire to help others benefit by my experiences, as herein set down. Many of my conclusions, you will of course realize, are purely hypothetical, yet I would feel myself to be a fraud of the first ranks if I took unto myself, either by direct statement or by innuendo, credit for those higher impulses which actually had to break down my own natural tendencies in order to get a foothold on me. Had I followed my intellectual conclusions and tendencies, I would have gone down in defeat at every one of those seven turning points in my life, a conclusion which I am forced to reach in the light of a reasonably sound interpretation of the meaning of the lessons which each of these turning points taught me.

Now let me summarize the most important lessons which I learned in my search for the rainbow's end.

First, and most important of all in my search for the rainbow's end, I found God in a very concrete, unmistakable, and satisfying manifestation, which is quite sufficient if I had found nothing more. All my life, I had been somewhat unsettled in my own mind as to the exact nature of that unseen hand which directs the affairs of the universe, but my seven turning points on the rainbow trail of life brought me, at last, to the conclusion which satisfies. Whether my conclusion is right or wrong is not of much importance; the main thing is that it satisfied me.

The lessons of lesser importance which I learned are these:

I learned that those whom we consider our enemies are, in reality, our friends. In the light of all that has happened, I would not begin to go back and undo a single one of these trying experiences with which I met, because each one of them brought to me positive evidence of the soundness of the Golden Rule and the existence of the law of compensation through which we claim our rewards for virtue and pay the penalties for our ignorance.

I learned that time is the friend of all who base their thoughts and actions on truth and justice, and that it is the mortal enemy of all who fail to do so, even though the penalty or the reward is often slow in arriving where it is due.

I learned that the only pot of gold worth striving for is that which comes from the satisfaction of knowing that one's efforts are bringing happiness to others.

One by one, I have seen those who were unjust and who tried to destroy me, cut down by failure. I have lived to see every one of them reduced to failure far beyond anything that they planned for me. The banker whom I mentioned was reduced to poverty, and the men who stole my interest in the Betsy Ross Candy Company and tried to destroy my reputation have come down to what looks to be permanent failure, one of them being a convict in the federal prison.

The man who defrauded me out of my $100,000 salary, and whom I elevated to wealth and influence, has been reduced to poverty and want. At every turn of the road which led, finally, to my rainbow's end, I saw indisputable evidence to back the Golden Rule philosophy which I am now sending forth, through organized effort, to hundreds of thousands of people.

Lastly, I have learned to listen for the ringing of the bell which guides me when I come to the crossroads of doubt and hesitancy. I have learned to tap a heretofore unknown source from which I get my prompting when I wish to know which way to turn and what to do, and these prompting have never led me in the wrong direction, and I am confident they never will.

As I finish these lines, I see on the walls of my study the pictures of great people whose characters I have tried to emulate. Among them is that of the immortal Lincoln, from whose rugged, care-worn face I seem to see a smile emerging, and from whose lips I can all but hear those magic words, "With charity for all and malice toward none," and deep down in my heart, I hear the mysterious bell ringing, and following it comes, once more, as I close these lines, the greatest message that ever reached my consciousness:

"Standeth God Within the Shadow of Every Failure."

⚡ ENTREPRENEUR ACTION ITEM
Make the Golden Rule Work for Your Business

Hill charts the course of his professional life, landing on a notion that should sound familiar: treat others as you wish to be treated. His use of the Golden Rule isn't glib here—it's purposeful and pointed, designed to impart that lesson to entrepreneurs who, too, are following a path of self-discovery against the backdrop of business.

When money is involved in your journey, what can encourage you to follow the Golden Rule and run an ethical business?

The Golden Rule is a way of improving emotional intelligence and increasing an awareness of ethics in every interaction, but it's no match for the common figure of the rogue business genius.

Just consider how lenient we are with individuals who are forging new ground, especially in areas such as technology or finance. And what about when businesses are unethical (as Hill portrayed in this essay)? Such bad actors set a bad precedent, and it can hold water for only so long before the dam breaks.

So, as Hill encourages here, be a force for good. The Golden Rule is one way to start doing that in your business. Here's how you and your business can adopt this concept productively.

Slow Change Through Social Intervention

Companies are beginning to realize that treating people well is essential to a long-term business strategy in a digitally connected world. Social media was the first wake-up call for businesses that quietly operated under unethical or simply poor values. The change is slow, but we are moving from the stick to the carrot, as the saying goes.

Before social media, advertising ruled. Wronged customers had two primary choices and little recourse otherwise: write a complaint letter or badmouth the company to friends, family, coworkers, and anyone else who would listen. That usually was the extent of it. Social media, however, offers the opposite extreme. We now live in an era of information overload. It's enough to make some people wish for the simplicity of early times, while others feel a sigh of relief that their complaints can make a difference.

Of course, each industry and its regulatory bodies have set forth their own standards. The Better Business Bureau (BBB) was formed in 1912 as a nonprofit organization that promoted honest advertising practices and resolved disputes between consumers and businesses. The BBB accepts complaints and serves as a mediator. Its truly revolutionary role, though, comes in the form of its business ratings. These scores consider the public's input, among other factors. Regulating agencies, on the other hand, keep a filter in place. A wall prevents people from seeing exactly what another consumer has said about a company or service.

Social media removes the barriers between customers and corporations. You now can see comments, ratings, and even photographic evidence of bad behavior not only online but in real time. (Those same tools can expose unfounded customer complaints, too). Treating customers poorly can have ripple effects.

Tangible Benefits

At first glance, the Golden Rule's financial impacts are simple. In fact, many companies include something along these lines in their values statements:

- Treat your employees as you would want to be treated, and they will work harder and stay with you.
- Treat your customers as you would want to be treated and they will come back again.

The Golden Rule provides guidance in hiring, too. Increasing numbers of employees want to work exclusively for organizations that have a positive impact on the world. As the millennial generation makes up an even larger proportion of workers in the coming years, companies will face mounting pressure to hold leaders and brands accountable—to associates and consumers alike.

When you treat your associates, customers, and the world well, you can maintain and build the loyalty needed to succeed in the long term. An unethical workplace also is a less productive one. According to another survey, almost 90 percent of workers who experienced incidents of unethical behavior while on the job stated they were personally affected. It distracted them from focusing on the task at hand.

Moreover, an ethical business avoids the sunk costs and bad press that can come with resulting legal issues. Companies can achieve the Golden Rule in part through transparency—a factor that equates to employee happiness, health, productivity, and ultimately, profit.

A Reminder of Ethics

How, then, do you make sure your business is on the right track? You can use the Golden Rule as a framework for all your decisions. When you stop to consider the other person, you practice empathy—and that's strongly tied to making ethical choices. *Psychology Today* contributor Mark B. Baer points us to several Harvard University studies and reports that attempt to understand the complex emotional connections between empathy and decisions. Those same sources uncover how fear and advertising can derail empathy.

Applying the Golden Rule activates your entire suite of ethical and emotional decision-making tools. This changes your day-to-day relationship with employees and clients as well as how you perceive the long view when weighing major, direction-setting alternatives.

You owe it to your business and yourself to keep the Golden Rule in mind at all times. Your associates, customers, bottom line, and collective conscience will reap the benefits in due time.

CHAPTER THREE

A Personal Inventory of the Seven Turning Points in My Life

I have often heard the expression, "If I had my life to live over, I would live it differently!"

Personally, I could not truthfully say that I would change anything that has happened in my life if I were living it over. Not that I have made no mistakes, for indeed it seems to me that I have made more mistakes than the average person makes, but out of these mistakes has come an awakening which has brought me real happiness and abundant opportunity to help others find this much-sought state of mind.

I am convinced, beyond room for doubt, that there is a great lesson in every failure, and that so-called failure is absolutely necessary before worthwhile success can be attained.

I am convinced that a part of nature's plan is to throw obstacles in a man's pathway, and that the greatest part of one's education comes, not from books or teachers, but from constantly striving to overcome these obstacles.

I believe that nature lays down obstacles in a person's pathway, just as the trainer lays down rails and hurdles for a horse to jump over while being trained to "pace."

So, I shall do my best to set down some of the lessons which my failures have taught me.

Every year I live, I am more convinced that a waste of life lies in the love we have not given, the powers we have not used, the selfish prudence that will risk nothing, and which, shirking pain, misses happiness as well.

Let us begin with my favorite hobby, namely, my belief that the only real happiness anyone ever experiences comes from helping others to find happiness.

It may be a mere coincidence that practically 25 of my 36 years were very unhappy years, and that I began to find happiness the very day I commenced helping others find it, but I do not believe so. I believe this is more than a coincidence. I believe that it is in strict accordance with a law of the universe.

My experience has taught me that you can no more sow a crop of grief and expect to reap a harvest of happiness than you could sow thistles and expect to reap a crop of wheat. Through many years of careful study and analysis, I have learned conclusively that that which you give comes back to you increased many times, even down to the finest detail, whether a mere thought or an overt act.

From a material, economic standpoint, one of the greatest truths I have learned is that it pays handsomely to render more service and better service than one is paid to render, for just as surely as this is done, it is but a question of time until one is paid for more than they actually do.

This practice of throwing one's heart into every task, regardless of the remuneration, will go further toward the achievement of material, monetary success than any other one thing that I could mention.

But this is hardly of less importance than the habit of forgiving and forgetting the wrongs our fellow humans commit against us. The habit of "striking back" at those who anger us is a weakness which is bound to degrade and work to the detriment of all who practice it.

I am convinced that no lesson which my life's experience has taught me has been more costly than the one which I learned by eternally exacting my "pound of flesh" and feeling it my duty to resent every insult and every injustice.

I am thoroughly convinced that one of the greatest lessons a person can learn is that of self-control. One can never exercise any very great amount of influence over others until they first learn to exercise control over themselves. It seems to me of particular significance, when I stop and consider that most of the world's great leaders were people who were slow to anger, and that the greatest of all the leaders through the ages, who gave us the greatest philosophy the world has ever know, as it is laid down in the Golden Rule, was a person of tolerance and self-control.

I am convinced that it is a grievous mistake for any person to start out with the belief that, upon their shoulders, rests the burden of "reforming" the world, or of changing the natural order of human conduct. I believe that nature's own plans are working out quite rapidly enough without the interference of those who would presume to try to rush nature or in any way divert her course. Such presumption leads only to argument, contention, and ill feelings.

I have learned, to my own satisfaction at least, that a person who agitates and works up ill feeling between people, for any cause whatsoever, serves no real constructive purpose in life. It pays to boost and construct instead of knocking and tearing down.

When I began the publication of this magazine, I commenced making use of this principle by devoting my time and editorial pages to that which is constructive and overlooking that which is destructive.

Nothing which I have ever undertaken in all of my 36 years has proved as successful or brought as much real happiness as my work on this little magazine has done. Almost from the very day that the first edition went on the newsstands, success has crowned my efforts in greater abundance than I had ever hoped for, not necessarily monetary success, but that higher, finer success which is manifested in the happiness which this magazine has helped others to find.

I have found, from many years of experience, that it is a sign of weakness if a person permits themselves to be influenced against a fellow human on account of some remark made by an enemy or someone who is prejudiced. A person cannot truly claim to possess self-control or the ability to think clearly until they learn to form opinions of their fellow humans, not from someone else's viewpoint, but from actual knowledge.

One of the most detrimental and destructive habits which I have had to overcome has been that of allowing myself to be influenced against a person by someone who was biased or prejudiced.

Another great mistake which I have learned by having made the same mistake over and over again, is that it is a grievous mistake to slander one's fellow humans, either with or without cause. I cannot recall any personal development which I have gained from my mistakes that has given me as much real satisfaction as that which I have experienced from the knowledge that I had, to some extent, learned to hold my tongue unless I could say something kind of my fellow humans.

I only learned to curb this natural human tendency of "picking one's enemies to pieces" after I began to understand the law of retaliation, through the operation of which a person is sure to reap that which they sow, either by word of mouth or by action. I am by no means master of this evil, but I have at least made a fair start toward conquering it.

My experience has taught me that that most people are inherently honest, and that those whom we usually call dishonest are victims of circumstances over which they haven't full control. It has been a source of great benefit to me in editing this magazine to know that it is a natural tendency of people to live up to the reputation which their fellow people give them.

I am convinced that everyone should go through that biting, though valuable, experience of having been attacked by the newspapers and losing their fortune, at least once in their lifetime, because it is when calamity overtakes a person that they learns who are their real friends. The friends stay by the ship while the "would-be's" make for cover.

I have learned, among other interesting bits of knowledge of human nature, that a person can be very accurately judged by the character of people whom they attract. That old axiomatic phrase "Birds of a feather flock together," is sound philosophy.

Throughout the universe, this law of attraction, as it might be called, continuously attracts to certain centers things of a like nature. A great detective once told me that this law of attraction was his chief dependence in hunting down criminals and those charged with breaking the law.

I have learned that the person who aspires to be a public servant must be prepared to sacrifice much and withstand abuse and criticism without losing faith in or respect for their fellow people. It is rare indeed to find someone engaged in serving the public whose motives are not questioned by the very people whom their efforts benefit most.

My experience has taught me that the person who accuses the world of not giving them a chance to succeed in their chosen work, instead of pointing the accusing finger at themselves, seldom finds their name in Who's Who.

A "chance to succeed" is something every person must go out and create for themselves. Without a certain degree of combativeness, a person is not apt to accomplish very much in this world, or acquire anything which other people covet very highly. Without combativeness, a person can easily inherit poverty, misery, and failure, but if you get a grip on the opposite to these, you must be prepared to "contend" for your rights.

The only "rights" a person has are those which they create for themselves in return for service rendered; and, it may not be a bad idea to remind ourselves that the nature of those "rights" will correspond exactly to the nature of the service rendered.

My experience has taught me that a child can be burdened with no heavier a load, nor visited with a greater curse, than that which accompanies the indiscriminate use of wealth. A close analysis of history will show that most of the great servants of the public and of humanity were people who arose from poverty.

In my opinion, a real test of a person is to give them unlimited wealth and see what they will do with it. Wealth which takes away the incentive to engage in constructive, useful work is a curse to those who so use it. It is not poverty that a person needs to watch—it is wealth and the attendant power which wealth creates, for good or for evil ends.

I consider it very fortunate that I was born in poverty, while in my more mature years, I have associated rather closely with people of wealth; thus, I have had a very fair demonstration of the effect of these two widely separated positions. I know I shall not need to watch myself so very closely as long as the need for life's ordinary necessities confronts me, but if I should gain great wealth, it would be quite essential for me to see that this did not take away the desire to serve others.

My experience has taught me that a normal person can accomplish anything possible of human accomplishment, through the aid of the human mind. The greatest thing which the human mind can do is to imagine. The so-called genius is merely a person who has created something definite in their mind, through imagination, and then transformed that picture into reality, through bodily action.

All this, and a little more, have I learned during these past 36 years, but the greatest thing I have learned is that old, old truth of which the philosophers all down the ages have told us, that happiness is found not in possession, but in useful service.

This is a truth which one can appreciate only after having discovered it for themselves.

There may be many ways through which I could find greater happiness than that which I receive in return for the work which I devote to the editing of this little magazine, but frankly, I have not discovered it, nor do I expect to.

The only thing I can think of which would bring me a greater measure of happiness than I already have would be a larger number of people to serve through the little brown-covered messenger of good cheer and enthusiasm.

I believe the happiest moment of my life was experienced a few weeks ago, while I was making a small purchase in a store in Dallas, Texas. The young man who was waiting on me was a rather sociable, talkative, thinking type of young fellow. He told me all about what was going on in the store—a sort of "behind the curtains" visit, as it were—and wound up by telling me that his store manager had made all of his people very happy that day by promising them a Golden Rule Psychology Club and a subscription to *Hill's Golden Rule Magazine*, with the store's compliments. (No, he didn't know who I was.)

That interested me, naturally, so I asked him who this Napoleon Hill was, about whom he had been talking. He looked at me with a quizzical expression on his face and replied, "You mean to say you never heard of Napoleon Hill?" I confessed that the name did sound rather familiar, but I asked the young man what it was that caused his store manager to give each of his employees a year's subscription to *Hill's Golden Rule*, and he said, "Because one month's issue of it has converted one of the grouchiest men we've got into one of the best fellows in this store, and my boss said if it would do that, he wanted all of us to read it."

It was not the appeal to my egotistical side which made me happy as I shook hands with the young man and told him who I was, but to that deeper emotional side which is always touched in every human being when he finds that his work is bringing happiness to others.

This is the sort of happiness which modifies the common human tendency toward selfishness and aids the evolution in its work of separating the animal instincts from the human intuition in human beings.

I have always contended that a person should develop self-confidence, and that they should be a good self-advertisement, and I am going to prove that I practice that which I preach on this subject by boldly asserting that if I had an audience as great as that which is served by *The Saturday Evening Post*, which I could serve monthly through this little magazine, I could accomplish more inside of the next five years toward influencing the masses to deal with each other on the *Golden Rule* basis, than all the other newspapers and magazines combined have done in the last ten years.

This, the December issue of the *Golden Rule*, marks the end of our first year, and I know it will not be construed as an idle boast when I tell my readers that the seeds which we have sown through these pages during these twelve months are beginning to sprout and grow throughout the United States, Canada, and some of the other foreign countries, and that some of the greatest philosophers, teachers, preachers, and businessmen of the age have not only pledged us their hearty moral support, but they have actually gone out and rounded up subscriptions for us in order to help foster the spirit of goodwill which we are preaching.

Is it any wonder that your humble editor is happy?

There are people who have more (much more) of the worldly wealth to show for their 36 years of experience than the writer has, but I have no fear in challenging all of them to show a greater stock of happiness than I enjoy as a result of my work.

Of course, it may be only a meaningless circumstance, but to me, it is quite significant that the greatest and deepest happiness which I have experienced has come to me ever since I began publishing this magazine.

"Whatsoever a person soweth, that shall they also reap."

Yes, it came from the Bible, and it is sound philosophy which always works. And my 36 years of experience has proven conclusively that it does.

The first time the notion ever struck me to own and edit a magazine, some 15 years ago, my idea was to jump on everything that was bad and pick to pieces all that I did not like. The gods of fate must have intervened to keep me from starting such an enterprise at that time, because everything that I have learned in my 36 years of experience fully corroborates the philosophy in the above quotation.

I ENTREPRENEUR TIP

The following passage, A Suggestion for Your Christmas List, is consistent with Hill's "extra mile" and "reap what you sow" philosophies that permeated his writings. He often used anecdotal passages like this to illustrate a point.

A SUGGESTION FOR YOUR CHRISTMAS LIST

Permit me to suggest a simple little service which you can render which ought to and probably would bring you great happiness and, at the same time, make others happy.

Go out and buy some Christmas and New Year's cards.

Write some sentimental little messages on these cards, in your own handwriting, then mail them not to your friends, but to your enemies. Send a card to everyone whom you ever disliked, and to everyone whom you believe ever disliked you. Make the message which you write on each card suitable for the person to whom you send it.

It will not hurt you to try this. It may do you much good. One thing sure, it will make you feel that you have been bigger, more broad-minded, and sympathetic this Christmas than you ever were before.

This is a year when concessions should be made by all of us. We have reasons a plenty for changing our attitude toward our fellowmen. We have been spared the yoke of "kultur" which menaced the world this time a year ago. We have stood at the graveside and watched old John Barleycorn as he was laid away forever. This and much more has happened which will make this a better world to live in.

You are not satisfied with yourself, anyway. That is a healthy condition, because no normal person is ever fully satisfied. You naturally want to make some change in your environment and in your habits for the new year that is approaching.

May it not be possible that you could do no better than to start in now, at the beginning of the year 1920, with a firm determination to cultivate tolerance, sympathy, forgiveness, and a sense of justice toward all your fellowmen, those whom you do not like as well as those whom you love?

May it not be an excellent idea to begin now to cultivate the habit of self-reliance, good cheer, and thoughtfulness for others, knowing, as you surely will know if you stop to think, that these same qualities will reflect themselves in those with whom you come in contact, and that they will eventually echo back to you in greatly increased measure?

We have all been narrow-minded, selfish, and stingy in years gone by. We have fed our mind upon hatred, cynicism, and distrust. We have wished our neighbors ill future; we have laughed when they were in trouble. Then let us forget these mistakes which we have made in the past, and just once, if for no other reason than to experiment, rise above our former selves and be big hearted and broad minded.

You cannot fill your heart with love and hatred at the same time. These two human emotions make uncongenial companions. One or the other usually dominates. Which, may I ask, would you prefer to dominate in your heart? Which, do you suppose, would ultimately serve you best and raise you to the highest point of achievement?

By all means, buy those Christmas cards and try the experiment which we have recommended. It will bring a ray of sunshine into your life that will touch every atom of your being and cause it to radiate those qualities which prompt the world to call a person "great."

True greatness is first manifested in one's own heart. The world never discovers the greatness until the individual themselves has discovered it. It may be a long while after you discover that you have risen above petty meanness, jealousy, hatred, and envy before the world discovers it, but one thing sure. This discovery will never be made by the world until it has been made by you.

When you begin to feel in the bottom of your heart that a great soul dwells within your body—that you have commended the process of transformation from the old self to the new—it will not be long until your fellowmen will commence making the same discovery.

You can make the first step in the direction of true greatness by sending out those Christmas cards to all whom you have disliked and all whom you believe have disliked you. It will require effort on your part to do this. You will have to overcome that damnable quality of stubbornness, but you can do it, and it will be worth doing.

We do not know for sure, but we strongly believe, that this experiment will be worth as much to you as anything that ever happened in your life, provided, of course, you are not already one of those rare souls who have risen above those negative qualities which stand between most of us and the opportunity to enjoy happiness and the only real success that can come to any human being—namely, the chance to bring happiness to others.

The biggest truth your editor has discovered in all of his experience is the fact that it pays in both dollars and in sereneness of mind to learn to forgive and forget the ingratitude and the unkindness of others. It is a wonderful thing to be able to feel and know down deep in your heart that you have risen above the common human trait of "striking back" and exacting your "pound of flesh" for every wrong done you. Just how wonderful it is you can only know by trying it. Then try it this Christmas, with the use of those Christmas cards.

WHY SOME PEOPLE SUCCEED

We have made an important discovery—a discovery which may help you, whoever you are, whatever may be your aim in life, to achieve success.

It is not the touch of genius with which some people are supposed to be gifted, which brings success.

It is not good luck, pull, nor wealth.

The real thing upon which most great fortunes were built—the thing which helps people rise to fame and high position in the world—is easily described: It is simply the habit of completing everything one begins, first having learned what to begin and what not to begin.

Take inventory of yourself covering the past two years, let us say, and what do you discover?

The chances are about fifty to one that you will discover that you have had many ideas, started many plans, but completed none of them.

You have heard it stated in axiomatic phraseology ever since you were old enough to remember, that, "Procrastination is the thief of time!" But because it seemed like a preachment, you paid no heed to it.

That axiom is literally true.

You cannot possibly succeed in any undertaking, whether it is large or small, important, or otherwise, if you merely think of that which you would like to accomplish and then sit down and wait for the thing to materialize without patient, painstaking effort.

Nearly every business which stands out prominently above the common run of similar businesses, represents concentration on a definite plan, or idea, from which there has been but little, if any, variance.

The United Cigar Stores' merchandising plan is built upon an idea, simple enough, but upon which concentrated effort has been directed.

The Piggly-Wiggly retail stores were built upon a definite plan, through the principle of concentration, the plan itself being simple and easy of application to other lines of business.

The Rexall Drug Stores were built upon a plan, through the aid of concentration.

The Ford automobile business is nothing more than concentration upon a simple plan, the plan being to give the public a small, serviceable car for as little money as possible, giving the buyer the advantage of quantity production. This plan has not been materially changed in the last twelve years.

The great Montgomery Ward & Company and Sears, Roebuck & Company mail order houses represent two of the largest merchandising enterprises in the world, both having been built upon the simple plan of giving the buyer the advantage of quantity buying and selling and the policy of "satisfying" the customer or giving him his money back.

Both of these great merchandising concerns stand out as mammoth monuments to the principle of sticking to a definite plan, through concentration.

There are other examples of great merchandising success which were built upon the same principle, by adopting a definite plan and then sticking to it to the end.

However, for every great success to which you can point, as a result of this principle, you can find a thousand failures or near failures where no such plan has been adopted.

This writer was talking to a man a few hours before writing this editorial—a man who is a bright and, in many ways, a capable businessman, but he is not succeeding for the simple reason that he has too many half-baked ideas and follows the practice of discarding all of them before they have been fairly tested.

This writer offered him a suggestion which might have been valuable to him, but he replied immediately, "Oh, I've thought of that several times, and I stared to try it out once, but it didn't work."

Note the words well:

"I started to try it out once, but it didn't work."

Ah, there was where the weakness might have been discovered. He "started" to try it out.

Reader, mark these words: It is not the person who merely "starts" a thing who succeeds. It is the person who starts and who finishes in spite of hell.

Anybody can start a task. It takes the so-called genius to muster up enough courage, self-confidence, and painstaking patience to finish that which they start.

But this is not "genius;" it is nothing but persistence and good, common sense. The person who is accredited with being a genius usually is, as Edison has so often told us, nothing of the kind—they are merely a hard worker who finds a sound plan and then sticks to it.

Success rarely, if ever, comes all in a bunch, or in a hurry. Worthwhile achievement usually represents long and patient service.

Remember the sturdy oak tree. It does not grow in a year, nor in two or even three years. It requires a score of years or more to produce a fair-sized oak tree. There are trees which will grow very large in a few years, but their wood is soft and porous, and they are short-lived trees.

The person who decides to be a shoe salesperson this year, then changes their mind and tries farming the next year, and then switches again to selling life insurance the third year, is more apt to be a failure at all three; whereas, had they stuck to one of these for three years, they might have built a very fair success.

You see, I know a great deal about that which I am writing because I made this same mistake for almost 15 years. I feel that I have a perfectly good right to warn you of an evil which may beset your pathway because I have suffered many defeats on account of that evil, and consequently, I have learned how to recognize it in you.

The first of January—a day for good resolutions—is nearing. Set aside that day for two purposes, and you will be quite likely to profit by having read this editorial.

First: Adopt a chief aim for yourself for the next year at least, and preferably for the next five years, and write out that aim word by word.

Second: Determine to make the first plank in that chief aim platform to read something after this fashion, "During the ensuing year, I will determine, as nearly as possible, those tasks which I shall have to perform from start to finish in order to succeed, and nothing under the sun shall divert my efforts from finishing every task which I begin."

Nearly every person has intelligence enough to create ideas in their mind, but the trouble with most people is that those ideas never find expression in action.

The finest locomotive on earth is not worth a shilling, nor will it pull a single pound of weight, until the stored-up energy in the steam dome is released at the throttle.

I ENTREPRENEUR ACTION ITEM
Maintain Accountability When Setting Your Goals

Most of us talk endlessly about our hopes and dreams, and our desire to achieve our goals. Yet, day after day, month after month, we put our ambitions on hold. We fail to take steps toward our objectives. We procrastinate.

You can have the greatest idea in the world and be brimming with talent and ambition, but unless you actually take steps to put those concepts to the test, you'll never know if you'll succeed or not. That's why it's so important to find ways to hold yourself accountable. Accountability keeps you striving toward your goals and reaching for your dreams. Accountability accelerates your performance by helping you make consistent, steady progress.

Stop dreaming and start doing by using these eight methods to hold yourself accountable to your goals.

Be Brutally Honest with Yourself

We're all naturally talented in some areas but struggle in others. For example, some of us excel at communicating through writing but struggle with face-to-face conversations. In order to hold yourself accountable to your goals, it's important to set goals that make sense—ones that emphasize and develop your strengths while also seeking to improve or minimize areas you're weakest in.

It's important that you make a brutally honest and thorough assessment of yourself—you need to see your talents and shortcomings as clearly as possible and understand what works best for you in reaching your goals.

What type of environment do you thrive in, and when are you most likely to fall short? Consider how you can improve your focus and efficiency in areas where you're shaky. Identify the factors that motivate you to stay on track.

Commit to a Schedule

One of the biggest missteps with accountability is setting deadlines for reaching your goals, but failing to set a schedule that will actually get you there. Often, we're so focused on the end goal (losing 20 pounds, writing a book, launching a business) that we forget that any goal can only be accomplished through a step-by-step process. We may hope, wish, and desire with all our heart, but it will never magically happen if we don't actually commit to making steady progress.

It's paramount that you set a schedule you can commit to. This will give you a game plan you can follow and a way to evaluate if you're consistently and persistently working toward your goals. Your schedule should set specific and time-oriented objectives, but they should be within reason. This will help you translate big goals into concrete, actionable steps.

For instance, let's say your goal is to increase followers and grow your base. Try setting a schedule to release fresh, quality content at least once a week. You commit to writing or producing an article, blog, or video every Friday, and come what may, you follow through. Once you start producing quality content, you'll start gaining followers and increasing your brand recognition—thus taking concrete strides toward achieving your goal.

Create Micro-Goals

You already know what your big dream is. You have an overarching plan and you've decided on a schedule. But chipping away at this mound of work can feel overwhelming—like a mountain that's too high to climb. This is where many people falter and get sucked into procrastination. Fight this urge and hold yourself accountable by making it as easy as possible to take baby steps in the right direction.

You can do this by breaking down each segment of your goal into a tiny "micro-goal." Divide each larger task into the smallest possible unit of progress, and include each of these baby steps in your schedule. Keep breaking down your goals until they're sliced up into tiny, easily achievable micro-goals. And make sure you take a moment to celebrate each small achievement.

Progress and accountability go hand in hand. If you make it easy to keep taking step after step, you're less likely to get overwhelmed and more apt to keep chipping away, holding yourself accountable to making progress.

Get an Accountability Partner

An accountability partner is someone who is committed to helping you reach your goals (and in turn, you'll do the same for them). If you're in a situation where you're working on goals independently, or you don't have a manager or a boss looming over you, having an accountability buddy will make you answerable to someone if you fail to follow through.

For instance, if you're trying to launch a new business or write a book, you're only accountable to yourself, and it may be easy to let your commitment slide. There's no one cracking the whip and making sure you're reaching your micro-goals and major milestones.

Having an accountability buddy works best if he or she is reliable and truly committed. It also works best when you both agree to use SMART goals (specific, measurable, attainable, relevant, and time-oriented). Your accountability partner may be able to give you unbiased feedback. If you can't find an accountability buddy, tell a friend or your family about your plans and ask them to help you stick to them.

Overcome Self-Sabotage

Self-sabotage is our subconscious way of limiting our success. It often springs from a fear of being pushed outside of your comfort zone. Self-sabotage is a self-destructive loop that smashes goals and kills dreams. If you have ever set goals and objectives for yourself, and then failed miserably to follow through, you've probably fallen into a pattern of self-sabotage.

In order to hold yourself accountable, you also have to understand what you're doing to impede your progress. Work to overcome self-sabotage by identifying your negative patterns. What are your triggers? How do you allow your fears to hold you back? Be on the lookout for ways in which you may be undermining yourself.

Know Your Why

Holding yourself accountable means having a crystal-clear reason why this goal is so important to you. How will accomplishing this goal improve your life or the lives of others? What is the value and purpose of this objective? Your accountability to your goal will be improved if you understand your motivations. That will help you build a positive mindset that reinforces why accomplishing this goal is important to you.

Keep your "why" top of mind when striving to reach your goals. Continue to educate yourself on your objectives—feed your mind knowledge and information that will build your "why" and help keep you focused.

Anytime you set an objective, you have to make a conscious effort to take the steps to see that goal through. Holding yourself accountable to your dreams means deeply embracing the reasons why those dreams matter and why you need to keep striving to reach them.

Celebrate Each Win

Taking time to celebrate each success you have—whether it be big or small—is an important part of holding yourself accountable because it helps you build momentum and stay focused. Each win builds your confidence—it reinforces your "I can do this" mentality.

Celebrating doesn't have to involve throwing a party or some other grand gesture. Everyday wins can be celebrated in small but meaningful ways that help you mark that moment in your mind.

Write down your daily or weekly successes. Put the list where you can see it every day, and keep adding to it so you can see how far you've come. Keep a master list of your goals and micro-goals, and cross off each one as you accomplish it. Take a moment to post it on social media (if it's something you feel like sharing). This will give your friends and family a chance to support and encourage you.

Review Your Progress

Last but not least, take time to regularly review the goals you're holding yourself accountable for. This is a chance to check in on your overall progress. A quick review of how far you've come can kick your motivation up a notch and get you back on track when you start to slide.

Take a look at how you're doing in keeping up with your schedule and accomplishing both your macro- and micro-goals. You should also ensure your accountability buddy is helping you stay on task. Are you pleased with your quality of work? Are you feeling good about your progress?

Look for areas where you can improve. Is your motivation slipping, and if so, what can you do to bolster it? The more empowered and excited you feel about your achievements, the easier it will be for you to hold yourself accountable to keep accomplishing those tasks and reaching your goals.

CHAPTER FOUR

When a Person Loves Their Work

Last night, I forgot to go to bed. I became so absorbed in my work that the silvery wings of early dawn had spread themselves over me before I noticed the passing of the night.

I feel refreshed. I feel able for the day's work ahead of me. The body building and body repairing process has been going on within me all night.

In producing this magazine and distributing it to the remotest parts of the country, we find it necessary to do much work that its readers never hear about. Organizing, preparing, and printing the material that goes into this magazine is the least of our work, and this seems more like play than it does work, because we love it. The hardest of our work is in the distribution of the magazine.

Night after night, week after week, we plan and execute, work and play, laugh and sing, speculate and prophesize, in the process of producing and distributing this magazine, but neither of us has ever complained of being tired.

After dinner, we walk five miles and back, for the necessary physical exercise. As we walk, we talk and we philosophize; we plan and think; we talk of the good there is in people and of the bad, with the soft pedal on the bad. Then we return to the playhouse where this magazine is created and play the game of helping people to see the joy and the beauty and the glory of cooperative effort that is based on the Golden Rule.

A few weeks ago, we had a chance to spend the weekend on a camping trip. We thought it over, saw ourselves fishing and enjoying the great outdoor scenery, but when we thought of the fun we could have right here among the tall buildings of Chicago, playing our game through the pages of this magazine, and helping thousands of others to enjoy our game, we decided we could not give up a whole weekend for so commonplace a game as that of fishing and hunting.

There is a psychological cause of this fact that a person never kills themselves by hard work if they are engaged in the sort of work they love. This principle can be demonstrated and proved by a score of simple illustrations. For instance, what boy is there who does not remember how long he could play baseball without ever growing tired, while ten minutes on the woodpile almost brought collapse.

Who can recall feeling the loss of sleep while they were spending the better part of the first half of every night with the person of their choice, while engaged in the work of trying to sell themselves to them?

Who can recall, without a desire for repetition, the hard day's climbing among the cliffs and rocks of a beautiful mountain range, with a party of picnickers, and who can remember ever having heard of such labor killing anyone?

Nature has so arranged things that where love and joy of service abide, there may be found, also, the reward of satisfaction. Also, nature has so arranged matters that the human mind repels all that it does not attract. There are only two forms of energy; one repels, and the other attracts. When the human mind is directing the physical body in an effort which it loves, the law of attraction is automatically brought into play, and the body finds the work easy, because there is no friction, no resistance from the law of repulsion.

Think for a moment and get this principle which I am trying to simplify, because it will pay you to do so.

Every act of the physical body which is the result of force of fear or necessity, and which does not arise out of pure love for the service to be performed by that act, immediately meets the resistance of the law of repulsion, and the result is friction, loss of energy, a tired body, and a tired mind.

When you drive a child to do a thing because it is afraid not to do it, then you set into motion the law of repulsion, and the result may be resentment that will bring on sickness or at least a big healthy cry, both of which wear out body cells and result in fatigue.

The same principle applies, of course, where people, out of necessity, are forced to engage in work which they do not love. They do it because they have to eat, but all the while, this law of repulsion is brought into action, and it is producing resentment, cynicism, fear, and other negative qualities, all of which tear down the tissues and the cells of the body and produce fatigue.

A laboratory testing which I made during the war showed what startling results could be produced by providing appropriate music for workers who worked under high tension and at high speed. They turned out from 25 percent to 50 percent more work, but this was not the best part of the discovery—they were not worn out when the day's work was over.

Surely here is a tip for the efficiency engineers and the employers of labor. Make work attractive, give it a touch of art wherever possible, and mix it with music; embellish it with any modifying influence that will disarm the law of repulsion, and the workers will do more and complain less, because they will not be worn out when the day's work is over.

To love praise, but not worship it, and fear condemnation, but not go down under it, is evidence of a well-balanced personality.

When I was a young lad, I used to attend those all-night social gatherings at which the young people of the community gather and dance and play games in the rural districts. Never can I remember having complained of being fatigued on account of loss of sleep or hard work, and these gatherings called for both. We worked very hard and slept not at all, but because the law of attraction was at work meanwhile, and the law of repulsion was not permitted to interfere, we came out of the night's work refreshed and ready for more of it the next night.

The physical body is an instrument upon which energy, which we call the mind, is constantly playing. If we so direct that energy that it does not arouse rebellion or bring into play the law of repulsion, there is no wear and tear on the body, and fatigue cannot be felt. But, when one set of emotions begin to claim the use of the physical body, and another set dispute that claim and try to repel the claimant, then war sets in between two opposing forces, and the result is death to body cells. They fall by the millions, like soldiers in warfare, destroyed because of lack of harmony of purpose and of effort between the body and the mind.

Humans are not the only ones who engage in warfare. There is a little war going on inside of every human body wherein peace and harmony and love to render service do not abide. Every act one performs that comes as a result of fear or necessity or any other cause than that of desire to perform the act, starts these two opposing forces of attraction and repulsion into motion, and the result is warfare and death, because the cells of the body are the physical beings through which these forces fight one another.

This is a scientifically proven fact that I am passing on to you, even though I have tried my best to strip it of scientific terms so it will be so obvious that all may understand and appropriate it.

For ten years, I have been analyzing people, and out of this research, covering the separate analysis of more than 12,000 people of varying ages, temperaments, and education, I have made the startling discovery that success in life—that eternal verity for which all mankind has been striving—is based upon a few very simple fundamentals, one of which is this:

That one will succeed in any undertaking if they love the work and learn how to bring into play the law of attraction and refrains from arousing the law of repulsion.

The system of character analysis which I worked out, as a part of my research work, covers more than 150 questions, and nearly every one of these is intended to bring out the nature of the work which the person being analyzed likes best. Once this fact has been established, it is as easy to write a prescription for success as it is to prescribe a remedy for a child who has a dirty face. In both cases, the patient often rebels and yells and tries to evade the remedy, but the prescription, when followed, does the work.

People succeed because they love their work, and no person can love their work if it is performed in a spirit of selfishness, with the object of squeezing the last drop of life blood from the person who purchases their labor. Success in life depends upon happiness, and happiness is found in no other way than through service that is rendered in a spirit of love. If service is not the end instead of merely a means to an end, happiness cannot be found in its performance.

Surely the World War should have taught us one thing, if it taught us nothing else, and that is the unquestionable fact that physical force cannot permanently succeed if it is of such a nature that it sets resentment and hatred into motion. Only truth and justice, based upon love for humanity and unceasing desire to place the interest of humanity above those of the individual, can permanently endure.

The person responsible for those misguided West Virginia miners taking up arms and trying to force their views upon the community was either a fool or a shrewd criminal whose only object was to further some interest—note that I said "some" interest—that was inimical to the interests of those who earn their living by the sweat of their brows.

I know the laboring people too well not to know that back of this fool's errand on which they started, there was a guiding mind of stealth and cunning, a mind that was actuated not by a desire to serve, but to profit selfishly, not to give but to get. Fellow workers of the world, permanent, desirable, constructive efforts cannot be produced in this way. There is a better way of getting that to which you are entitled, and unless every promise of every sound leader of the past, and every conclusion of the great philosophers, and every promise that is written in the growing trees and the flowing brooks and the singing birds and the faces of little laughing children, by the divine hand that guides the destiny of this universe, is false and unsound. This better way may be found at the round table, where people meet and take each other into their confidence, give and take, make allowance, and ask for allowance, basing their negotiations always on the Golden Rule.

⚡ ENTREPRENEUR TIP

Negotiate with the Golden Rule in mind. Instead of going into a negotiation anticipating the worst outcome, remind yourself that you are not there to spar, but to reach a middle ground where both parties give a little.

Force will win for a time, but force does not make a person love their work, and unless they do love it, they will surely miss the greatest of all that life on this earth promises, which is the joy and the peace of mind and the happiness that comes from harmonious, friendly relationships with others.

Find the work you love, forget yourself in that work, and your reward in both satisfaction and monetary consideration will be ample for your needs on this earth, with a safe margin left over.

⚡ ENTREPRENEUR ACTION ITEM
Lead with Passion

Hill's article here focuses on a couple of key takeaways. First, that finding work you love to do is a reward that impacts other areas of your life. Second, he notes that your outlook on work can have a far-reaching effect on how you negotiate, advocate, and participate in your company's culture. He speaks from the employee's point of view, but the message resonates for leaders as well.

Sometimes, the bad moments in leadership can seem so overwhelming that leaders lose their passion and love for their people and work. But what does passion really mean? Passion is when you put more energy into something than is required to do it. More than just enthusiasm or excitement, passion is ambition that is materialized into action to put as much heart, mind, body, and soul into something as is possible. Passionate leaders motivate and inspire their people to be the best they can be and put as much of their best selves as they can into achieving their goals. Passionate leaders are able to share their ambition with others and inspire them to go after the same goals. Simply put, passionate leaders and managers make a lasting difference.

Unfortunately, leaders can't always stay passionate about work. According to leadership expert Dan Black, some of the reasons that passion for leadership dwindles include:

/ The stress and demand of a project or task causes you to burn out.
/ The weight of leadership takes a toll on you over the years.
/ Personnel problems or issues weigh heavy on your shoulders.
/ A significant situation or issue happens at home.
/ You failed in a major leadership role at work.

When you're burned out and discouraged, your love and passion for work suffers. Your efficiency lessens, and you can be short-tempered with co-workers — and even friends and family. But don't worry. There are ways to rekindle your passion and love for your work.

Set Goals

Passionate leaders always have a vision — it's what they are passionate about. In order to stay focused, leaders must have specific goals that they are committed to accomplishing. Every step toward their vision must be specifically laid out. It's easier to stay committed when you have a clear direction. It also helps lessen the stress and demands of a project. When you set goals and share the vision with your team, you also reinforce a team mindset among your employees.

Celebrate Each Goal

It's hard to remember the importance of your vision when all you do is work on it. You need to acknowledge the progress of your goals and recognize the contributions that you and your team make. Give them, and yourself, the needed pat on the back to further ignite your passion and theirs. Celebrating the little things can remind you that what you're doing is going somewhere and isn't just some endless task you have to do. When you celebrate each achievement, you show that you're getting closer to your vision.

Share Accountability

The task isn't yours alone. If you are a leader, your job is to guide your team — but each member of the team has their own purpose. Empower your team to reach their full potential by trusting them to do their part. Be clear about your vision and share information that is essential to your team. But while it's important to have control over a project, you can't control everything. Trust your team to do their best in their respective tasks. This can help ease the burden of leadership from your shoulders.

Have a Support System

Sometimes, self-motivation fails; we all inevitably tire out. In your personal life, it's good to have a partner or friend that you can talk to about your day. When you have someone to talk to, the burdens of leadership are easier to deal with. Also, look for a mentor from outside your organization. Many professionals are people that needed an outlet and perspective away from their company. It's been said that you can't see the picture if you're in the frame. Sometimes, you need someone who can offer perspective without being involved. Someone on your team might be geared up when you're not; ask them to be the motivator for the day. It's OK to let someone else step up on your unmotivated days. Someone needs to keep the passion going, and your co-worker might be able to energize you as well.

Maintain Work-Life Balance

Being passionate at work doesn't give you an excuse to overwork. If anything, it's more of a reason for you to take a break so that you don't run out of passion and love for what you are doing. When your passion dwindles, your productivity and even your personal life can suffer. You creativity is depleted easily when you're overworked, too, so make sure to find ways to restore your energy and passion, be it a hobby that you enjoy or something else that lets you relax, unwind, and recharge.

Use these tips to rekindle your passion and motivation for leadership.

CHAPTER FIVE

Initiative

A little boy was the immediate cause of my writing this. I write about him for several reasons, and as far as I can tell, the least of these is the fact that he is our son—his mother's and mine.

Be it remembered he is only one of our three sons.

But, my subject is initiative.

Wherever I see a person exercise that rare quality called initiative, whether that person be man or woman, child or grownup, I always feel like lending that person encouragement to repeat the performance. Perhaps, then, the real object of this article may be to encourage this little chap when he grows older and turns back the pages of this magazine and reads that which his Daddy wrote years before. Perhaps, also, I may be writing as a means of encouraging other little chaps, and some who are no longer so little, to emulate this little fellow's example.

At any rate, here is the story:

Someone has said that all people are born equal. I challenge that statement. In fact, I can disprove it beyond any question of doubt. All people are not born equal. All have equal rights to enjoy freedom after birth, which, of course, is a far different matter from being born equal.

From early childhood, some children are highly educated, and by "educated," I mean that they have the ability to get that which they want. They have strategic ability. They know how to make use of the law of self-preservation.

Other children have not such ability. Some of these later acquire it, by training, while others never do. It always has been and perhaps always will be a nice question as to whether training enables a child to acquire the needed ability to protect its interests, or whether training merely develops that which is quietly slumbering within the child, waiting to be aroused and put into operation. It is not my purpose to answer this question, but merely to raise it for you to think about as you read.

The little fellow about whom I am writing is my namesake. To be perfectly formal and proper then, meet Master Napoleon Blair Hill, financier, businessman, and all-around in economic problems (also in managing fathers and mothers).

A few months ago, Blair wanted to go into the newspaper business. His mother had one set of notions about the proposed enterprise, while his father had still another.

I wanted to see all of our boys experience that wonderful thrill which comes to a child when they feel, for the first time, that they are doing something on their own responsibility. I wanted to push him off the rail into deep water so he could learn to swim, so to speak. Like the old eagle that takes the eaglets to the edge of the cliff and pushes them over that they may learn to use their wings, I wanted to see Blair go into the newspaper business and get his toes stepped on by older boys and turned away by the grownups who see nothing in a little new merchant except a waif of the streets and many other thrills, all of which, from the viewpoint of a father, would have been good and necessary experience for him.

While his mother and I were talking the matter over from day to day, Blair made matters much easier for both of us by exercising some of that rare quality called initiative. One night while we were away, he went to the neighborhood shoemaker, an Italian gentleman with whom he was on good friendly terms, and negotiated a loan of six cents.

He took this capital and invested it in newspapers. He sold his stock, repeated, sold out again until he was too tired to work any longer; then he returned the capital he had borrowed and made his way homeward with his profits—47 cents.

In one evening, without previous experience, without counsel and without advice, on borrowed capital, this little chap earned within three cents of as much as I used to earn for a whole day's work when I was more than twice his age.

When his mother and I got home that night, we heard the story of this unusual business success. Blair was in bed, asleep, but the housekeeper gave us the details. We went into Blair's room. The little fellow was sleeping on one hand. His mother removed the hand from under his head, opened up his dirty little paw, and nickels and pennies rolled all over the room.

He was taking no chances on losing that hard-earned money, so to bed with him it went.

Blair's mother crawled around over the floor, gathered up those pennies and nickels, and placed every one of them back in his hand, then knelt by his bedside, and cried as if her heart would break.

Blair's transaction affected me differently, though. The significance which I attached to it was this: That come what would, here was one of our boys who would always be able to earn his way. I saw leadership in my child, and I was proud, very proud of that ability. I saw one thing while his mother saw something else.

Blair's mother saw a tired little boy who had been wagging a bundle of newspapers around over the dangerous streets, facing all sorts of danger. I saw a proud little businessman whose first enterprise had been a huge success, and the experience of which would give him greater courage and more faith in his ability in his next effort. It was all a matter of viewpoint and previous emotional experiences. His mother had inherited and experienced from contact with life one set of emotions, while I had inherited and acquired an entirely different set; consequently, the self-same transaction appealed to each of us in different manner.

> ⫽ **ENTREPRENEUR TIP**
>
> Embrace the point of view of those around you—even if you don't necessarily agree. Want to voice your disagreement in a productive way? Start by validating the opinion of the person with whom you disagree. To do this, you can use phrases like, "I see you point that . . . ," or "I hear you saying . . ." Then, instead of focusing on how "right" you are, talk about how you feel about or understand the issue using phrasing like, "That makes me feel . . ." or "I think our disconnect may be about . . ." Using phrases like these allows you to humanize the issue and reach a place of understanding instead of trying (and often failing) to "win" the argument.

I laughed when those nickels and pennies rolled out of our child's hand; his mother wept. I laughed because, well, maybe because I thought one person was enough to be weeping in the house at one time.

As I took my wife in my arms and gently led her away from her happy, slumbering child, I kissed the tears away from her cheeks as I told her what a wonderful businessman our little fearless boy would grow up to be, and in my heart, I felt glad that God made mothers just as they are, ever ready to shed a tear for every living thing that suffers pain and hardship.

EDITOR'S NOTE: *Hill uses the story of his own child's business instincts to showcase how differently we perceive initiative. For him, the topic was framed around the concept of family and how he and his wife interpret the child's actions differently. In the next passage, Hill frames initiative not around having a brain full of information, but around having the skillset to seek and find that information. The questionnaire he mentions is in reference to a widely-circulated series of questions that Thomas Edison was believed to have asked prospective employees. Edison created several versions of his famous questionnaire that catered to the specific job for which he was seeking employees.*

Mr. Edison's Questionnaire

Yes, I took a fling at Thomas A. Edison's test questions.

The result was interesting. From off-hand memory, I answered a little better than 5 percent of the questions, and no more.

Long pause while you have your laugh at my ignorance!

Laugh heartily, because we do not mind being laughed at; besides, laughing is one of the finest mental tonics on earth.

Now if you are through with your side-splitting exercise, settle down and read carefully for a few minutes, and I will do my best to have a little laugh with you, only I'll laugh last!

I took Mr. Edison's entire list of questions, as it was published in the public press, strolled over to the public library, and in exactly half an hour, I had correctly answered 95 percent of the questions. With two telephone calls, one to the department of chemistry of a local university and the other to one of our daily newspapers, I got the information with which to answer the other 5 percent, the entire performance consuming less than three quarters of an hour.

I believe many a person who tried to answer those questions and fell down, just as I did when relying on memory, failed to get the real significance back of the questions and failed, probably, to learn the practical lesson which those questions taught, namely, that education consists not in facts stored away in one's own mind, but in knowing where and how to get facts quickly when needed.

Ninety-five percent of the questions on Mr. Edison's list called for information which in no way has any bearing on my life's work; consequently, I had no real reason for carrying the necessary facts with which to answer them around in my mind.

I soon learned, after entering law school, that no person could hope, nor was anyone expected, to carry all the law around in their head. I found that the purpose of law training was to teach a person how to get the particular point of law they wanted, when wanted, and to be able to apply the right principle to the legal procedure in hand.

Now this same rule applies in all walks of life. Education consists of the ability to get whatever one needs with which to successfully carry out their chosen life's work, and any knowledge beyond this is excess baggage, dead material, and might just as well be left in the encyclopedias, public libraries, and the archives of the institutions of learning.

True education consists of self-analysis that you may find out what sort of a temperament you have, what work you are best fitted to perform, and the ability to gather up the proper tools with which to do it. College degrees are no evidence, per se, that those holding them are educated. Neither is lack of a college degree evidence of ignorance or illiteracy.

A college graduate recently applied to one of the great metropolitan newspapers for a job. For the purpose of ascertaining how much knowledge of a general nature he had, he was asked what he knew about Socrates, to which he replied, "nothing," but he quickly added, "I know where to find out." He was told to go and find out and report back the next day, prepared to tell all he knew concerning the life of Socrates.

He went to the public library and worked all afternoon and well into the night, gathering data concerning the subject at hand. Next day, he reported back at the newspaper office, at the appointed hour, with one of the finest biographical sketches of the life of Socrates that the editor had ever seen.

The man was given the job, even though he knew nothing about the newspaper business, and today, would you believe it, that man is one of the highest-paid newspaper people in America and one of the most successful people in the business.

He carried no facts around in his head concerning Socrates, but he knew where to get those facts when needed.

To become an accurate thinker, you must separate facts
from information and distinguish between important and
unimportant facts.

Incidentally, while I am on this subject, let me mention three of the very best sources from which facts can be secured concerning practically all that mankind knows or ever has known, as far as known facts have been recorded.

One is the public library, one is any modern university, and the other is any modern daily metropolitan newspaper office. In the office of a newspaper, for example, you can secure accurate data on practically any subject. For example, I wanted the address and the exact whereabouts of ex-President William Howard Taft a few days ago. The *Chicago Examiner* supplied it in less than five minutes, and furthermore, they rendered me this service courteously and willingly, as if it gave them real pleasure to do so.

Most of the big daily newspapers have on file the pictures of most of the leading people of affairs of the world, and these can be seen or even borrowed by responsible people, as a part of the service which the great newspapers are rendering the public.

It is surprising what a variety of accurate facts one can secure, for the asking, from the professor in a modern university. If you wish facts concerning chemistry or botany or biology or electricity or any other subject, you can usually secure all or at least a part of that which you wish by merely calling on the professor of one of these departments at your local university.

The person who succeeds in life is the person who gets what they need when they need it, and if they do not get it, they are not a success, no matter how proficient they may be in explaining the reason why they did not get it.

If I were testing out applicants for positions (with all due apologies to my good friend Edison), I would ask them not a question as to what they knew. I would be more interested in finding out what they could do with what they already had, and if they knew where to get facts when needed.

Abraham Lincoln was not an educated man, as far as schooling went, nor was he a person of letters; yet he was powerfully adept at getting things done when and in the manner necessary. He knew nothing about geometry or chemistry, but he knew considerable about the human heart and the ways of mankind.

He knew how to get people to cooperate with him, even though they actually disliked and disagreed with him. Lincoln was a man of education.

Not long ago, a college professor asked me this question:

"What would be the first thing you would do if you were elected President of the United States?"

"The first thing I would do," I replied, "I would surround myself with a cabinet of the most successful executives I could find, each of whom knew where to find out quickly that which they did not already know."

Careful analysis of the modus operandi of people who have succeeded to an extraordinary degree, in business, finance, or industry, will disclose this one fact, that all such people succeeded, not as a result of the fact which they had stored up in their own minds, nor as a result of their own efforts, but they succeeded because they knew how to select people who could get things done. They succeeded because they recognized the fact that no person has a complete master mind, but that such a mind can be built to order, assembled, as it were, through the right sort of combination of other's minds.

> ## *I* ENTREPRENEUR TIP
>
> Surround yourself with people smarter than you. Don't underestimate the power of brainstorming when you need to think of possible solutions to your problem. Getting your team around the conference room table and opening your minds to multiple possible solutions (no matter how far-fetched) just might open the door to one that really works.

Mr. Edison probably would not employ any applicant for a job, even though they could actually answer all of the questions on his list, unless that person showed clearly that they had the ability to get the fact with which to answer any question which might not be on the list, and also the ability to take any combination of facts and work them into a practical plan. Possessing facts does not mean that those who possess them know what to do with them.

For example, in my research work a few years ago, I met a graduate of Yale who had come down to begging on the streets. He possessed one of the most remarkable collections of facts that I have ever heard of one person possessing, yet he was as helpless as a child when it came to building these facts into a practical plan through which to earn a living.

If a person applied to me for a job, I would much prefer that they be able to satisfy me that they possessed certain qualities not brought out in Mr. Edison's list of questions, for example:

I would want to know that they understood the value of initiative and actually practiced it; that they believed in themselves; that they had a good sense to create an atmosphere of harmony among those with whom they worked; that they had developed the habit of performing more service and better service than they actually contracted to perform; that they refrained from slandering those whom they did not like; and last, but not least, that they knew when, where, and how to get all the necessary facts and materials with which to perform his work efficiently.

Such a person, in my opinion, would come far nearer being a person of real education than the person who could merely answer all of Mr. Edison's long list of more or less abstract questions.

Mr. Edison's list of questions reminds me of a man down in Washington, D.C. who was taking the civil service examination for the position of mail carrier. One of the questions, obviously placed there to test the applicant's general knowledge, was this:

"How many soldiers did the British send over here to put down the rebellion of 1776?"

To which the applicant replied, after scratching his head and thinking a moment (with emphasis on the word "thinking"), "A damned sight more than ever went back."

He passed the examination with flying colors and got the job. His answer showed that he had a keen sense of humor and was quick to do the practical thing in the event of an emergency.

So, do not lose sleep if you tried to answer Mr. Edison's list of questions and did no better than I. Try again, with the aid of the local library, and you will run up a better score.

⚡ ENTREPRENEUR ACTION ITEM
Build Your EQ to Boost Your IQ

What Hill points out with these stories about initiative and intelligence is that both are linked not only to how an entrepreneur views themselves, but more importantly, how they navigate the world. That might involve how you, as a business leader, might think perceive struggle and success or how you might position your own knowledge or lack thereof. His theories speak to our modern notion of emotional intelligence (EQ).

There are many types of intelligence and emotional intelligence, even though it's much discussed these days, is often not displayed much in the workplace. Being able to pinpoint and manage emotions (both yours and others') is what helps you better manage relationships. It can be a rigorous process to cultivate being more open to watching your own emotions, but this work will lead to a happier and more successful life.

In order to be emotionally intelligent, you need to be self-aware. For example, some leaders fake their self-confidence and may not even realize it. There's a big difference between true self-confidence and faking it. People you work with can subconsciously feel the difference. You work more competently when you have realistic self-confidence. This is because you understand your feelings and you can tell when a strong emotion is about to occur, so you adjust. Understanding your feelings sounds pretty basic but it's actually something that takes people a long time to learn.

Someone who is emotionally intelligent is resilient, able to remain calm under pressure. When you do get upset, you get over it quickly and don't dwell on it. You're the go-to person in a crisis, which is an obvious leadership trait. You're also emotionally balanced, you keep distress in check, and you don't let it spill over to others around you. Leaders like this tend to keep an eye on longer-term goals no matter what bumps may occur along the way.

Emotional intelligence also requires empathy, both emotional and cognitive. You truly understand the feelings and perspectives of others. This lets you see things from many angles and people pick up on this. Seeing how someone feels lets you communicate better. People like this also tend to be good listeners, pay attention better, and don't just wait for their turn to speak.

Emotional intelligence is both an innate trait and a learned skill. Pick the areas below where you're the weakest and strive to improve on a daily basis. If you're prone to being in your own bubble and like working alone, you may need to push yourself to achieve more emotional intelligence. Try these seven tips to get started:

Surround Yourself with Higher Emotional IQs
They say birds of a feather really do flock together. To some extent, you are the average of the people you have around you the most. Make an effort to be with people you admire and who have qualities, including emotional intelligence, you want to emulate.

Read More
It really is that simple (it can also include audiobooks). Reading books designed to increase your emotional intelligence will do just that. Take in a book while you drive, do tasks that don't require a lot of headspace, or even while you run.

Practice Active Listening

Humans don't naturally actively listen, instead we wait our turn to talk. Consciously listening takes work. You have to stop yourself while someone is talking and notice if you're actually formulating your response instead of listening. This takes time to learn. The rewards are nice though. Active listening increases compassion and empathy—pillars of emotional intelligence.

Learn from Your Mistakes

We hear so often that we should learn from our mistakes that we take this for granted or forget to do it. One way to build this skill is to write down past mistakes or failures, then pinpoint what went wrong and what you can learn. If you don't take the time to observe these things, you'll just keep repeating them.

Choose Leisure Activities Wisely

Find activities that you truly enjoy which also happen to increase emotional intelligence. It might be a chess club, meditation group, yoga, or a book club. Lean away from watching too much TV. Down time doesn't need to be "brain turned off time."

Embrace Lifelong Learning

We should never stop learning, but education doesn't have to take place in a traditional school classroom. How are you actively learning something new in the moment? What do you want to learn? Rock climbing? Singing? Aikido? The options are endless.

Take Care of Your Mental Health

Mental and emotional health are intimately connected to your physical health. It's widely accepted that people feel better when they have an emotional outlet in the form of another person. Professional therapists are tremendously valuable because they offer a non-judgemental space for people to speak about what's happening their lives. If for some reason you can't bring yourself to see a therapist, at least have someone in your life you can speak to regularly about your feelings.

Emotional intelligence takes work and practice just like any other form of intelligence. Good news—you're in total control of working those emotional intelligence muscles. Watch who you interact with, learn new things, and give yourself emotional outlets. These will all help grow this highly valuable personal capability.

CHAPTER SIX

Permanent Success

The magazine which you hold in your hands is the best sort of evidence that adversity is a blessing in disguise, because it owes its birth to adversity and temporary failures.

The finest thoughts which will find their way into print in these pages are thoughts which were born of struggle and hardship.

Turn back the pages of history, back to the very beginning of all that we know of civilization, and you will find that the men and women whose names lived after they passed on were those whose efforts were born of struggle, hardship, and failure.

People may leave behind them monuments of marble without struggle, hardship, and failures, but those who would build monuments in the hearts of their fellow people, where neither the disintegrating forces of the elements nor the degrading hand of humanity can destroy them, must pay the price in sacrifice and struggle.

Ten years ago, a baby was born in one of the wealthiest families in America. The whole world showered the little fellow with gifts which it did not need and could not use. One foolish king sent, as his offering to the useless collection, a gold crib that cost $40,000.

I was going to law school in the city where that baby was born; therefore, I know considerable about the event. That bountiful shower of gifts reminded me that like attracts like. Wealth attracts wealth, and poverty attracts poverty. It is the way of human nature.

By and by, this little baby grew old enough to be taken on the streets. When he was taken out, he was flanked by a coterie of servants and private detectives whose business it was to see that no misfortune overtook him. Never in all this baby's life was he permitted outside the protecting influence of these servants. He could not go on the street alone. He was watched over with care that would lead one to believe that he might have been made of superior clay.

This little fellow had no cares. He experienced no hardships. He never knew what struggle meant. All he knew was that he was not born to toil. He did not have to dress himself; he had servants for that purpose. He did not have to use his eyes; he had servants' eyes to use. He did not have to use his hands; he had servants' hands to use. In fact, he did not have to do anything.

Each winter, he went with his army of servants to play in the rolling waters of the warm Gulf of Mexico, where he was not bothered with the cold blizzards of the north. When he went out to swim, he was surrounded by this same army of servants, who flanked him and watched to see that no harm befell him.

Two years ago, this little fellow, now a boy of 10 years, had just returned to the north from his wintering place in Florida. He was out in the gardens with his servants when he noticed that the gates were open, and he saw beyond, that much longed-for freedom that every normal child is constantly seeking. While the servants' vigilance had slackened for a moment, he saw his chance and made a run for the streets. He got outside and into the middle of the streets when he was run down and instantly killed by a Ford automobile.

At the very moment that this was happening, there were no less than a million little urchins, located in the crowded streets of the great cities, not one of which could have been run down by an automobile in an open 10-acre field, because these little "unfortunates" had learned the art of self-defense! Out of struggle—struggle borne of necessity—they had learned to get out of the way of automobiles.

Verily do we repeat that, out of struggle and hardship, comes endurance and power.

Servants and private detectives can watch over a baby, and possibly keep him from being stolen; they can even keep him from being run down by automobiles, if they attend to their duties properly, but the eternal law of compensation takes its toll when the little fellow grows up to maturity and commences to take his place among men. He pays dearly for the early protection which relieved him of struggle. The very first time he is called upon to rely entirely upon his own resources, he finds that he has no real "resources."

The strong-armed blacksmith developed his strength out of "resistance." The greater the resistance, the greater his strength. By wielding a heavy hammer day in and day out, he finally grew a mighty arm that serves him wherever physical strength is needed. He developed his strong arm in exactly the same manner that all strength must be developed, by overcoming resistance.

We point with pride to Lincoln as being one of the really great Americans of the past, yet how many stop to consider that his strength, both physical and moral, grew out of hardship and struggle. No doubt Nancy Hanks would have given Lincoln as royal a birth as that of the little boy mentioned above, if she had been financially able, but if she had done so, there is but little doubt that Lincoln would never have risen to the heights to which he attained.

Much of Lincoln's greatness grew out of his early struggles and hardships, because out of these grew strength, that mighty strength which carried him through one of the most trying crises of this country.

The most dangerous handicap with which any child could be surrounded is the handicap of money, provided it is used to relieve the child of struggle.

Twenty odd years ago, I was secretary to a wealthy man whose two sons were away at college. It was a part of our duty to make out a check for $100 for each of these boys on the first of the month. This was their "spending money," and spend it they did!

Well do we remember how we envied these boys the easy time which this monthly remittance provided. By and by, they returned home with their "sheep skins" and other things, too, among them being the capacity for great quantities of whiskey.

One of those boys is now under the sod, and the other is in an insane asylum.

Last year, we had the privilege of speaking in the college where one of the boys went to school. The principal of the school told us that the $100 check which came monthly for that boy was the influence that undermined him. With that check, he had money to be a "good fellow." This led to his drinking habit, and that led to ruination.

We can see, now, that fate dealt us a lucky blow when it placed the great cosmic urge of necessity behind us, in our early childhood, and forced us to struggle for a schooling and for existence itself. That struggle seemed hard then, but we know now that it was the strengthening process which we needed to prepare us for our work in life.

Our own boys are coming along now, and in spite of the powerful moral which we have drawn from our own experience and from our observation of the two boys mentioned, we see ourselves inclined to "make it easy" for our boys when we can. This is a common tendency—a human sort of tendency, perhaps—which can lead nowhere but to distress and grief when the child is called upon for the reserve strength which is not there because they have never met with the necessary resistance.

It may seem like a trite statement, but it is nonetheless true on that account, to say that the only permanent good that can come to a child comes out of that which they do for themselves. The greatest service that can be rendered any person on earth is the service which causes that person to rely upon themselves.

We met a man in Lawton, Oklahoma, on our recent tour of the country, who gave us much food for thought. We had ridden around with him all afternoon in an automobile before we learned that he was stone blind. His dark glasses covered his eyes, and not a sign of his affliction was to be seen on his face or detected from his voice. He laughingly carried on one of the most interesting conversations we have ever listened to, and entertained us so splendidly that we did not notice his blindness.

Afterward, we learned of this man's early struggles. He had lost his eyes at the age of 4. Several years ago, he presented himself at Northwestern University, in the city of Chicago, for matriculation as a student. The officials refused to accept him, urging him not to undertake a stiff course such as tried the strength of able-bodied young men and women to the utmost.

But this young fellow knew no defeat. He was persistent. Finally, the university officials asked him how much money he had with which to pay his way through school, and he replied, "35 dollars!"

They told him he would only be wasting his time to start in school with his handicap without sufficient funds, and advised him not to try it. He went out and walked around the block a time or two and then came back and said, "Now, look here, let me enter for the first semester, and if I do not keep up with my classes and pay my way, you can turn me out." They consented, largely, we suspect because they did not have the heart to refuse.

This young man not only completed the first semester with honors, at the head of his classes, but he finished the entire course, leading all the way through.

But this is not all! Brace yourself on your chair for a shock!

He paid his way by taking notes in the lecture rooms, transcribing them on the typewriter, and selling copies to his fellow students, those who had two perfectly good eyes and money in the bank besides.

Rarely does a person ever have opportunity to test the limits of his ability. We can accomplish pretty much whatever we make up our minds to accomplish. If we are not forced to test our strength, through dire necessity, through struggle, through hardship, we seldom discover our possibilities. Lay it down as a general rule—and a sound one at that—that real strength comes from struggle, hardship, adversity, and handicaps imposed upon us by causes beyond our immediate control. If we could "control" these causes, they would not exist because we would eliminate them, thereby depriving ourselves of the most beneficial experience that can come to a human being.

Twenty odd years ago, this writer found himself forced to work as a laborer in the coal mines. Nothing short of necessity would have induced him to perform such work, yet, out of that very work, came experience that has played and is now playing no small part in the very best service which he has rendered and will continue to render his fellow humans. We are in the midst of a great industrial crisis, not alone in America, but throughout the world, and much of our effort is directed toward the elimination of the "cause" out of which this crisis grew. Our efforts have not been without visible results, something that would not have been possible except for the "forced service" rendered in the coal mines years ago, which brought us close to the people who labor in those mines and gave us a splendid chance to study the conditions under which they work, the grievances of which they complain, their faults, and their virtues.

Now, when we presume to write for or about those who perform the most lowly sort of labor, we write, not as one whose hands were never covered with the grime and dust of honest toil, but as one who has worked shoulder to shoulder with these people whose voices are now crying out for justice and fair treatment.

And when we send back the message to the laborers out of whose ranks we came, urging them to "perform more work and better work than actually paid for," we know that we are not leading them astray or counseling them unwisely, because it has been this one practice, more than any other, which has helped us to throw off an undesirable, unprofitable environment and get into the work we love. The reason why this is sound practice is obvious. It develops greater and greater ability until, finally, a person just naturally bursts out of their cramped environment by attracting the attention of people in a more desirable walk of life. Out of effort and resistance comes strength! The greater the effort, the greater the compensating strength, and the person who foolishly withholds the best service which they are capable of rendering because they may not be receiving what it is worth, is only prolonging the time of failure.

I know of no other single quality that has paid me greater dividends and carried me further toward my ultimate goal in life than has that of the habit of performing more service and better service than was actually paid for!

But, lay stress on that word *habit*.

This practice must become a habit, and recognition must be gained before the real results begin to show. To merely perform more service and better service than is paid for one day and refrain from doing it the other five working days of the week would be something like training one hour a week for a prize fight and resting the remainder of the time.

> / **ENTREPRENEUR TIP**
>
> Foster good habits for success. Simple meditation is a terrific way to center your thoughts and prepare for the day to come or even to step out of your busy day and reconnect with your thoughts. You don't have to have a special room or complicated process. Just find a quiet spot, empty your mind, focus on breathing, and just be for a few minutes. Then, your mind is clear and ready to tackle the next thing on your to-do list.

A person may be "born to the weary treadmill of toil," but if they understand that out of toil, out of resistance, out of effort, out of adversity comes strength, they will not long remain a victim of this handicap. Instead, they will soon burst the cords of circumstances and environment, no matter how strong they may seem, and rise to claim their own that is born of struggle and hardship.

A TOAST TO FAILURE

As my fingers begin to play upon the keyboard of my typewriter, I look and see before me a great army of people whose faces show the lines of care and despair.

Some are in rags, having reached the last stage of that long, long trail which all people fight to avoid—failure.

Others are in better circumstances, but the fear of starvation shows plainly on their faces, the smile of courage has left their lips, and they, too, seem to have given up the fight.

The scene shifts, I look again, and I am carried backward into the events of history past, and there I see, also, the failures of the past—failures which have meant more to the human race than all the successes recorded in the history of the world.

I see the homely face of Socrates as he stood at the very end of that trail which people call failure, waiting, with upturned eyes, through those moments which must have seemed like an eternity, just before he drank the poisoned hemlock.

I see, also, the face of Thomas Paine, the person whom the English sought to capture and put to death as the real instigator of the American Revolution. I see him lying in a filthy prison in France, waiting calmly under the shadow of the guillotine, a reprieve from death and writing—as he waited—many pages dedicated to the advancement of human liberty.

And, I see, also, the face of the person from Galilee suffering on the cross at Calvary, the reward for his efforts to interest people in being decent with one another here on earth.

Failures, all!

Oh, to be such a failure. Oh, to go down in history, as these people did, as being brave enough to place humanity above the individual and principle above pecuniary gain. On such failures rest the hopes of the world.

ENTREPRENEUR TIP

Failure isn't the end of your story. Failure gives you the chance to stop and take stock of what you want and where you want to go next. When you fail, it's your chance to imagine a new path for yourself.

The measure of a real person is in their ability to see, with clear eyes, all the beauty and the good and all the injustice and the wrong there is in the world and still maintain an even sense of proportion in all things, toward all people.

Every adversity is a blessing in disguise.
Our failures of today become the foundation stones of success
tomorrow, if we properly interpret them.

I bow to the person who can see the imperfections of mankind without becoming cynical; who can temper justice with mercy; who can see the good there is in people who disagree with them; who can work in harmony with those whom they do not admire; who exercises self-control and lets reason instead of emotion govern their actions toward others.

Such a person was the immortal Lincoln.

He was a person with a message when he had sufficient provocation to have become a man with a grievance instead.

As a reward for his greatness, the world has erected an everlasting monument to Lincoln's name, a monument that the elements can never disintegrate, a monument that no depredating hand can destroy, a monument built in the heart of the people - built, not of stone, but of love, sympathy, patience, tolerance, and forgiveness for mankind—those gentle qualities which memory attaches to his name—and which are now, as always, the real test of a man.

THE DAMAGING EFFECTS OF SUBTERFUGE AND DECEIT

Nothing really seems to be very bad until someone tries to cover it up through subterfuge and deceit.

We may not agree with the person who boldly admits their shortcomings, but we cannot withhold from them a certain healthy respect on account of their boldness.

On the other hand, the moment a person resorts to secrecy or to subterfuge, even in connection with matters of small importance, that person becomes immediately marked as unworthy of trust.

If there is a skeleton in the closet which is apt to crawl out to plague one, at the most inopportune time, a mighty good plan is to voluntarily drag it out and say, "There it is; what are you going to do about it?"

People will forgive most anything unless there is an attempt to cover it up and clothe it in secrecy. In that event, forgiveness comes reluctantly, if at all.

Many a solid friend has been made by open frankness in connection with matters which, within themselves, were of small importance, while on the other hand, life-long enemies have been made by lack of this frankness.

If a person is secretive and resorts to deceit and subterfuge in small matters, the supposition is that in matters of greater import, the same tactics will prevail.

EXCEED EXPECTATIONS

This simple injunction comes from a person who started at the very bottom, in the lowliest sort of labor.

It constitutes the keynote of almost every public address this person delivers; it permeates nearly everything he writes; it creeps into his everyday conversation.

There are many reasons why this is sound counsel, only one of which need be mentioned, namely: every person who forms the habit of delivering this sort of service soon attracts the attention of competitive bidders for their services. They stand out above the common crowd like a skyscraper above the ordinary buildings, and there is keen competition for their labor.

Give the best service you know how to render, regardless of the amount you receive for it, and soon, much sooner than you might imagine, you will become a "marked" person, and greater responsibilities and higher wages will be thrusting themselves upon you.

Deliver the best services you can, not necessarily out of consideration for the purchaser, but out of consideration for yourself. Failure to practice this habit is the chief obstacle that stands between 95 percent of the people and success, but of course this does not apply to you, or does it?

Aimlessness is a sin, and it leads straight to poverty, misery, want, and failure. A person without a definite, constructive purpose in life is simply one of nature's mistakes, because they did not intend to create such a being, in all probability.

⅃ ENTREPRENEUR ACTION ITEM
Embrace and Bounce Back from Failure

Hill is arguing here that grit and determination are most often products of imperfection. No one's journey to entrepreneurship is perfect—far from it, actually. And that's a good thing. After all, the lessons you learn along the way are only made possible from the struggles you face, from the failure you experience.

Entrepreneurship is an ongoing series of ups and downs. Whether you're a newbie banking on each and every sale and loss or a veteran dealing in big numbers and packages—this journey is anything but stable and easy.

Of course, we love what we do. And it makes the rollercoaster totally worth it. But that doesn't take away from the intensity of tough emotions we face when failure does hit. Whether it's a big client proposal that ended in a no, a longer phase of feeling scarcity in your company or a publishing deal you were sure you had and fell through at the last minute, these moments of failure aren't easy.

We all face these moments. It's inevitable and every failure is a learning opportunity. The question becomes not how can we avoid failure but rather how can we get an energetic rebound when we are in a total slump. Or how can we best learn from this failure to succeed better next time?

If you have hit a wall and feel like you've been knocked down, you have a choice. Either let it take a serious toll on your confidence, drive, and energy or get back up and turn things around. You take the lessons and the experience, you take care of yourself, and use all of it to make you better moving forward.

Here are five steps that can help you get back on track and bounce back even stronger:

Be Aware of Your Self-Talk

When you fall into self-judgment, criticism, or even bad habits like name calling or labeling yourself, you'll end up held down with negative energy. We're all way too hard on ourselves.

Instead of letting that inner dialogue run the show, take note of it, and take a moment to give yourself some empathy. Try congratulating yourself on something you've done well recently and breathe into the fact that you are a human being with wins and losses. And this too will pass. The Mayo Clinic published a study titled *"Positive thinking: Stop negative self-talk to reduce stress,"* in which they explain that negative self-talk is detrimental to your stress management and even your health, citing a longer lifespan and better cardiovascular health. They also discuss ways to identify negative thinking and put positive thinking into practice.

Ask for Support

Every entrepreneur needs a network of people they can trust and can call when they feel low. This is essential to success. If you don't have it already, focus on putting together a collective of people who love you—the kind of people who don't compete with you and who love and honor you. Take a moment to think about who these people are for you. And when you're struggling, don't be shy to reach out and get support.

One option for creating this support system is to consider joining a mastermind of like-minded entrepreneurs or one who are in a similar industry. A mastermind is defined as "a peer-to-peer mentoring concept used to help members solve their problems with input and advice from the other group members." The concept of a mastermind group was actually introduced by Napoleon Hill in his 1925 book, *The Law of Success*. Focus on finding a mastermind group which best fits your specific goals and industry.

Take Some Space

Sometimes we need to step away from our businesses to gain perspective. Take a day off work, and go golfing or to the spa. Give yourself little a break from all of the noise and stress. Ideally, build activities into your regular schedule which allow you to reorient and recharge—then get back in the game. When you make a practice of taking nourishing breaks, the failures won't feel so tough.

A famous example of someone taking a longer break and coming back stronger than before is when Steve Jobs left Apple. When he rejoined the company, they skyrocketed.

Start a Journaling Practice

On a particularly rough day, your journal can be the ideal outlet. Write down all of your thoughts, and be real about what you're feeling. No need to filter yourself there. It'll feel good to put your feelings into words.

Writing is powerful because it has been proven to boost your mood, help you manage stress, lower symptoms of depression, and even improve your memory. Check out these and many more amazing benefits of journaling in this article from the Positive Psychology Program.

Ask Good Questions

One of the practices you can employ in your entrepreneurial path is to ask good questions like, "What is this really teaching me?" Or, "What am I aware of that I'm pretending not to be?" When you come from a space of inquiry instead of assumption, suddenly you can see beyond the chaos of your mind and get some clarity and perspective.

When it comes to failure, it's important to remember that you are not alone. Everyone will reach a low point in their business at some point. Who you're being to yourself and how you handle these low points will have a direct correlation to how you get back up and come back better than ever.

The beautiful thing about entrepreneurship is that we're always willing to try something new and different. With this mindset, the possibilities are limitless. If you're struggling right now, try these steps and trust that you'll get back up sooner than you think.

CHAPTER SEVEN

The Magic Ladder to Success

"The Magic Ladder to Success" has been delivered in practically every city in the United States, in a personal lecture, before hundreds of thousands of people. There is an indescribable "something" about it which attracts, holds, and inspires all who hear it. It has helped thousands find their first step toward achievement. It appeals alike to the rich and the poor, the educated and the illiterate, and has the effect of bringing people together in a spirit of closer understanding.

The object of this ladder is to show what is personal power, and how it is developed in those who do not possess it to achieve success in any endeavor. Personal power comes only through *organized knowledge intelligently directed.* Facts within themselves do not represent power. Knowledge, unorganized and without intelligent control and direction, does not represent power. There is a great deal of knowledge carefully classified and stored away in a well-edited encyclopedia, but it represents no power until it is *transformed into organized, intelligently directed effort.*

There is no power in college degrees, nor in the education which these degrees represent, until it is classified, organized, and put into action.

Human power is organized and intelligently directed energy, as presented by facts, intelligence, and the faculties through which the human mind operates.

In weight, tensile strength, and size, there is a strong log chain in a sack full of disconnected chain links, but these links represent only a potential chain until they are organized, connected up, and the links welded together. So it is with a person's faculties. They must be organized before they represent power.

There are two kinds of personal power. One is represented by the organization of the individual faculties, which gives increased power to the individual, and the other is represented by the organization of individuals and groups of individuals.

A little handful of well-organized soldiers have been known to put to rout ten times their number of disorganized, undisciplined ones, and history is full of the biographies of people who have risen to fame and fortune through the process of organizing and intelligently directing their individual faculties, while millions around them, with equal opportunities, remained mediocre or out-and-out failures.

There is considerable energy in an ordinary small electric dry battery, but not enough to do bodily damage if one should form a short circuit with their finger and absorb the entire charge. A thousand such dry batteries are equally harmless *until they are organized and connected together with wires.* Through this process of organization, if the energy of the entire thousand batteries is fed to one wire, enough energy is produced to turn a considerable piece of machinery. This group of dry batteries may be likened to individuals in that greatly increased power that comes through the organized effort of a large group of people, as compared to the efforts of the same people acting singly.

The object of this ladder, mainly, is to direct attention to the modus operandi through which individual power is developed and applied to the economic problems of life.

If you will *organize* your own faculties after the pattern laid down in this ladder, by properly developing the qualities represented by the 16 rungs, you will find your power enormously increased. You will find yourself in possession of power which you did not know that you possessed, and through the intelligent direction of this power, you can attain practically any position in life to which you aspire.

The sixteen rungs of this ladder represent the choicest and the most illustrative experience of my 21 years of business life and research. They are:

Rung #1	A Definite Aim in Life
Rung #2	Self-Confidence
Rung #3	Initiative
Rung #4	Imagination
Rung #5	Action
Rung #6	Enthusiasm
Rung #7	Self-Control
Rung #8	Exceed Expectations
Rung #9	Attractive Personality
Rung #10	Accurate Thought
Rung #11	Concentration
Rung #12	Persistency
Rung #13	Failures
Rung #14	Tolerance and Sympathy
Rung #15	Work
Rung #16	The Golden Rule

I will take you behind the curtains of my own private life that you may learn these great lessons, as portrayed in the outline of the ladder, with the hope that the road over which you will have to travel, to reach the objective for which you are striving in life, may be somewhat shortened, and the obstacles which will surely await you somewhat minimized.

Success ought not to be a mere matter of chance, as is true in the majority of instances, because the roadway over which success is reached is now well known, and every inch of it has been carefully and accurately charted.

The Great Mental Ladder to Success will carry you wherever you wish to go if you will master it and organize your faculties according to its plan, a statement which I make after having not only organized my own faculties and directed them to a given end successfully, but after having helped others to do the same in many thousands of cases.

This Great Mental Ladder to Success represents twenty-two years of actual experience and observation, at least 12 of which have been directed to the intense analysis and study of character and human conduct. I, during the past twelve years, have analyzed more than twelve thousand people. These analyses developed some startling facts, one of which was that 95 percent of the adult population belong to the class which might properly be called "unorganized" (both as to individual faculties and as to group or collective effort) or followers, and the other 5 percent might be called "leaders". Another startling fact discovered from organizing and classifying the tendencies and habits of human beings, as shown by these analyses, was that the main reason why the overwhelmingly large percentage of people belonged in the class of followers was lack of a definite purpose in life and a definite plan for carrying out that purpose.

❘ ENTREPRENEUR TIP

Map out your plan to success by setting intentional goals. As you set your goals, remember to keep them SMART: Specific, Measurable, Achievable, Relevant, and Time-Bound.

With the foregoing analysis of the Great Mental Ladder to Success, you have already seen that the ladder deals entirely with the subject of acquiring personal power through organization, coordination, and classification of the human faculties.

Bear in mind this fact, that this ladder is not intended as a panacea for all the evils which beset the pathway of the human race, nor is it intended as a "new" formula for success. Its purpose is to help you organize that which you already have and direct your efforts in the future more powerfully and more accurately than you have done in the past. Its purpose, stated in another way, is to help you educate yourself, meaning by the word educate, to develop, organize, and intelligently direct your natural faculties called the mind.

Power comes through real education.

No person is educated who has not learned to organize, classify, and intelligently direct the faculties of their mind to a definite end. No person is educated who has not learned to separate facts from mere information, weaving the facts into an organized plan.

Mere schooling is no evidence of education. College degrees are no evidence, per se, that those holding them are persons of education.

The word *educate* comes, if we recall correctly, from the Latin word *educo*, meaning to develop from within, to educe, to draw out, to expand through use. It does not mean to cram the brain with knowledge, as most dictionaries tell us that it does.

I dwell at length on this word-educate and on the word-organization because these two words are the very foundation, the very warp and woof of the Great Mental Ladder to Success.

Education is something which you must acquire. No one can give it to you. You must get it for yourself. You have to work to get it and you have to work to keep it. Education comes not from knowing, but from doing. The *Encyclopedia Britannica* is full of facts, but the books themselves have no power. They are not educated because they cannot put into action the facts which have been classified and filed away in their pages. So it is with the human automaton who merely gathers knowledge and makes no organized use of it.

There is a considerable energy in a ton of coal, but the coal must first be dug out of the ground and put into action, through the aid of combustion, before that energy can be utilized. That which is merely latent in the human brain represents no more energy or power than does the coal under the ground, until it is organized and put into action to some definite end.

The reason that a person can acquire an education through the cooperation of schools and teachers, more readily than they can acquire it without these, is the fact that schools help to organize knowledge.

If we seem to lay undue stress upon this question of organization, let us remind you that lack of this very ability to organize, classify, and intelligently direct the faculties of the mind constitutes the rocks and reefs on which a large majority of the "failures" flounder and go down to ruin.

If, through repetition and by approaching this question from various angles, as we have intended to do, we can drive home the importance of properly organizing your faculties and directing them to a definite end, we will have done for you all that any school on earth aims to do for its students.

I know beyond room for doubt that any person of mature mind can take this ladder and rapidly assimilate the plan upon which it is built, then use these principles for the purpose of developing, in his or her own mind, those necessary qualities out of which success may be easily and rapidly attained.

The sixteen rungs of this ladder tell us what we must have before we can reach success. There is nothing mysterious, nothing technical about either the ladder or the lessons on The Science of Human Behavior. These principles are available to all who care to make use of them. You do not need anything or anyone as a means of helping you make use of these principles. As a matter of fact, *you*, only, are the person who can use them to your advantage.

It was not intended that the order in which each subject is placed on the ladder indicate its importance, or the point at which it should be developed as a quality. Many of these subjects bear an equal importance to the whole, and it would be hard to say which should come first.

With the foregoing as a prelude, we are now ready to take up the first rung of the Great Mental Ladder to Success.

RUNG 1: A DEFINITE AIM IN LIFE

The selection of a definite chief aim must necessarily be the first step to be considered, because this is the architect's plan from which you will work in transforming your objective in life from the idea stage to reality. It is the mariner's compass which keeps you headed in the direction in which you wish to travel.

The selection of a specific chief aim is the point at which most people falter, hesitate, and finally stand still in a quandary as to which way to go or what to do.

This is one of the main reasons why most people accomplish so little in life. They have nothing definite in mind and, consequently, there is nothing definite in their action.

No one would think of gathering together a quantity of sand, lumber, brick, and building materials with the object of building a house without first creating a definite plan for that house, yet your author's experience in analyzing over 12,000 people prove conclusively that 95 percent of the people have no such plan for building a career, which has a thousand times more importance than the building of a house.

Do not overlook the significance of the word "definite," because it is the most important word in the phrase "a definite aim in life." Without this word, the sentence represents that which we all have, which is nothing more than a vague aim to succeed. How, when, or where we know not, or at least those of us who belong to the 95 percent class do not. We resemble a ship without a rudder, floundering on the ocean, running around in circles, and using up energy which never carries us to shore because we do not aim toward one *definite* goal and carry on until we reach it.

> *The person who has a definite aim, and a definite plan for attaining it, has already gone nine-tenths of the way toward success.*

You are commencing, now, to acquire personal power through the organization, classification, and intelligent direction of knowledge, but your first step must be the choice of a *definite* aim, or else you might as well have no power since you will not be able to guide it to a worthwhile objective.

It is necessary not only to have a *definite* aim in life, but you must also have a *definite plan* for attaining that aim. Therefore, place on paper a written statement of your definite aim and also a written statement, in as much detail as possible, of your *plan* for attaining that aim.

There is a psychological reason for insisting that you reduce your *definite aim* and your *plan* for attaining it to writing, a reason which you will thoroughly understand after you have mastered the subject of auto-suggestion. This reason is explained, again, in another article that will appear in these pages on the subject of self-confidence building.

Bear in mind that both your *definite aim* and your *plan* for attaining it may be modified from time to time. As a matter of fact, you will be an unusual person if you have the vision and the imagination to see a *definite aim* now that will be large enough in its scope to satisfy your ambition a little later on. The important thing for you to do, now, is to learn the significance of working always with a *definite aim* in view, and always with a *definite plan*. This principle is one that you must make a part of the process of organizing your faculties, and you must apply it in everything you do, thus forming the habit of systematic, organized effort.

Memorize this written statement, and each night, just before you go to sleep, affirm to yourself over and over again, many dozens of times, that you will attain the object of your chief aim. The scientific explanation of exactly what takes place when you do this is given further along in the lessons of applied psychology and auto-suggestion; therefore, we will not enter into that subject at present. You now have the idea back of the adoption of a chief aim in life and all the instructions necessary as to how to make this idea effective in your own life. Do not stop to ask such questions as this: "Will it really do what you say it will? Will it really work?" The thing for you to do is to *try it out and see for yourself.*

This writer takes full responsibility for the statement that it positively will work, not sometimes, but always. Do not expect it to work in a day if the objective which you have set out to reach requires several years for its natural development, however.

We offer you no magic wand, nothing mysterious, nothing occult, no miracle-performer, but simply a common-sense plan, such as a person would want if they started to build a house and wished to know before starting how much material to buy and what the house would look like after it was completed. They would do exactly what we have instructed you to do, namely, draw a definite plan before they started.

One year from the time that you write out your first statement of your *definite aim in life*, you will be surprised, more than likely, at the small scope it covered, for you will then have developed greater vision and greater self-confidence, and you will be able to accomplish more because of your belief that you can do so, and because of your courage in setting a bigger task for yourself, as indicated by your *definite aim.*

This process of "education," of educing, expanding from within, drawing out your mind, will enable you to think in bigger terms without becoming frightened. It will enable you to look upon your *definite aim* in life with eyes of analysis and synthesis, and to see it, not only in its entirety, but in its component parts, all of which will seem small and insignificant to you. Engineers move mountains from one spot to another with no difficulty whatsoever, not by trying to move the whole mountain at one shovel-full, you understand, but by shovel-full at a time, according to a *definite plan*.

The time and the necessary money required with which to build the Panama Canal were correctly estimated years ahead, in fact, before a single shovel-full of dirt had been removed, because engineers who built it had learned how to work by *definite plans*.

The Canal was a success.

It was a success because the people who planned and built it followed the principle which your author has laid down, for your guidance, as the first rung in this ladder; therefore, you can readily see that there is nothing new about this principle. It needs no experiment to provide its accuracy because the successful people of the past have already proven this.

Make up your mind, now, what you wish to do in life, then formulate your plans and commence doing it. If you have trouble deciding what your life work ought to be, you can secure the services of able analysts (not many of them, but there are a few) who can assist you in selecting a life work that will be in harmony with your natural inclinations, temperament, physical strength, training, and native ability.

RUNG 2: SELF-CONFIDENCE

It would hardly be worthwhile to create a *definite aim* in life or a plan for attaining it unless one possessed the self-confidence with which to put the plan into action and achieve the aim.

Nearly everyone has a certain amount of what is ordinarily considered self-confidence, but only a relatively small number possess the particular kind of self-confidence to which we have referenced, as constituting the second rung in the Magic Ladder to Success.

Self-confidence is a state of mind which anyone can develop in a short period of time. The modus operandi through which this is done is set out in detail in a lesson of self-confidence which will appear later, but we will take up, now, the task of making plain the necessity of this quality.

Lack of self-confidence is probably the widest of the chasms which yawn between a person and the attainment of their chief aim if they have one.

The negative quality called lack of self-confidence is one of the things which causes a person to refrain from adopting a definite aim after the necessity for doing so has been placed in their mind.

The main difference between Henry Ford, who created a very concrete chief aim put it into action, and John Henry Smith, who formerly worked alongside of Ford in a machine shop, is practically nil excepting on two points. Namely, Ford created a chief aim and developed the self-confidence to put it into action, and John Henry Smith did neither.

Education consists of doing—not in merely knowing!

The difference in results between Ford's twenty years of efforts and those of John Henry Smith's is considerable and amount to millions of dollars which Ford owns, versus zero which Mr. Smith owns.

It was largely a matter of self-confidence that caused Lincoln to try for the presidency of the United States. Most of us would have said, "Oh, well, I'm nothing but an uncouth rail splitter; what's the use of my trying for the greatest office in the United States. I couldn't be elected."

But Lincoln believed in himself, created a chief aim, and won.

That's all there was to it.

Self-confidence does two things—it inspires you on to greater effort, and it impresses those with whom you come in contact with your earnestness and will power.

Years ago, I was engaged as a laborer in the coal mines. I was without a *definite aim* and lacked the self-confidence necessary in creating such an aim. Something happened one night which marked the most important turning point in my life. I was sitting before the open fire, discussing with the man with whom I lived this very problem of problems that has now come up to plague the entire world—the spirit of unrest and antagonism between employer and employee. I said something which impressed this man, and he did something which gave me my first lesson in self-confidence building— he reached over, took me by the shoulder, looked me squarely in the eye, and said, "Why, you are a bright boy. And if you will get out and go to school, you will make your mark in the world."

It was not what he said as much as it was the manner in which he said it—the sparkle in his eye—the firmness with which he gripped my shoulder as he spoke, which impressed me. That was the first time in my life that anyone had told me that I was "bright," or that I might make my "mark" in the world. It gave me my first ray of hope, my first fleeting glimpse of self-confidence. The seed of self-confidence was sown in my mind on that occasion, and it has been growing all these years. The first thing this planting in my mind of the seed of self-confidence did was to cause me to break away from the mines and enter more remunerative work. It caused me to become thirsty for knowledge, so much so that I am becoming a more efficient student every year that I live, until today when I can gather, classify, and organize facts in less than one-tenth the time required only a few years ago.

RUNG 3: INITIATIVE

Initiative is that very rare quality which impels a person do that which ought to be done without being told to do it. All great leaders must possess initiative. A person without initiative could never become a great general, either in warfare or in business and industry, because generalship, to be successful, must be based on intense action.

Golden opportunities are lurking at every corner, waiting for the person with initiative to come along and discover them. When a person performs only the tasks allotted to them and then stops, they attract no particular attention. But when they take the initiative, go ahead and look for other tasks to be performed after their regular duties have been taken care of, they attract the favorable attention of their superiors who willingly allot to them greater responsibilities, with pay accordingly.

Before a person can rise very high in any field of endeavor, they must become a person of vision, who can think in big terms, who can create definite plans, and then carry these plans into action, all of which makes it imperative that the quality of initiative be developed.

One of the significant features concerning this magic ladder is the extent to which its rungs blend and harmonize with one another, to the end that the whole ladder constitutes a powerful organization of usable material.

In developing the quality of initiative, it is absolutely necessary to form the habit of doing every needful thing at the time when it ought to be done. Procrastination is a sure antidote for initiative. A putter-off never gets on. It is a remarkable fact, however, that all who have developed self-confidence and who have established a chief aim, have a strong tendency toward initiative, if in fact they have not already developed this faculty in sufficient quantity.

You can easily see how closely connected are the qualities of self-confidence and initiative, and just how the development of both of these is aided by the creation of a well-defined chief aim. One blends into the others. They are all connected and closely related, being attached to one another as the links of a chain, each link forming a necessary part of the whole. You will see that not a single subject laced in this ladder could be eliminated any more than a link in a chain could be eliminated without impairing the strength and the completeness of the chain itself.

RUNG 4: IMAGINATION

Imagination is the workshop of the human mind in which old ideas are built into new combinations and new plans. When Edison invented the incandescent light, he merely brought together, in his imagination first, and then in his laboratory, two well-known principles and hooked them up, so to speak, in a new way. He knew, as almost every amateur electrician knows, that friction in an electric line would cause heat, that the line could be heated, at the point of friction, to a white glow and thereby produce light. But the trouble was that the wire would burn in two. Finally, after searching all over the world for a special fiber or filament that could be heated to a white glow without its burning in two, Edison thought of the old charcoal principle, wherein a pile of wood is placed on the ground, set on fire, and then covered over with dirt and the air cut off. The wood smolders along, but it cannot burn up entirely because most of the oxygen has been cut off, and there can be, therefore, not enough combustion. The moment Edison thought of this charcoal principle, he went into this laboratory, placed the filament inside of a globe, cut off the air, and lo! he had produced the long sought incandescent light.

When Gutenberg turned his attention to the invention of the modern printing press, he also made profitable use of initiative and imagination, because he gave wings to thought which carries the happenings of the world to our door each day, at a cost of 2 or 3 cents, and brought the whole world into closer intercourse.

When the Wright Brothers turned their attention to the airplane, they used initiative and imagination which, within the span of a few years, mastered the air and shortened the distance between two given points by an enormous proportion.

Imagination is the process of creating, in one's mind, a picture. And the material out of which this picture is created is the previous sense impressions which have been implanted in the brain, through one or more of the five senses.

You cannot imagine anything which does not represent a picture that is built out of parts of other things which have been planted in your mind.

Had humans never seen birds flying in the air and fish swimming in the sea, they never would have invented either the submarine or the flying machine, because there would have been no material in his mind out of which to create them.

Nothing is ever constructed by humans in concrete physical form until after a picture of it has been first created in their minds. The building of such a picture is called imagination.

Sunshine is good—only mushrooms grow without it. Yet, in the production of great people and women, the north wind, rain and storm, and stinging disaster and agony have also played a part.

You can easily see how you must use your imagination in creating a chief aim. You do this by seeing yourself in possession of the thing or the station in life which is the object of your chief aim.

In developing self-confidence, you can see how necessary it will be to make use of your imagination. You will never occupy a higher station in life, and you will never achieve more than you imagine you can. Your progress toward your chief aim will never get ahead of your imagination; remember that. To the contrary, your imagination must precede your progress, and to the extent that you make your imagination vivid and back it up with a strong desire to reach your objective, will success crown your efforts.

We have now made the first four rungs of the Great Magic Ladder to

Success, and we can easily see, as we stand on the fourth rung, how closely intertwined these four rungs are, how they dovetail, how necessary every one of them is. Now comes the fifth step.

All of the great inventions owe their existence to the blending of these two forces, initiative and imagination. The limits to which a person of ordinary ability can attain, through the use of initiative and imagination, no person can define.

Lack of these two qualities is the main reason why 95 percent of the adult people of the world have no *definite aim* in life which, in turn, is also the reason why this same 95 percent constitute the followers in life.

Leaders are always people of initiative and imagination.

RUNG 5: ACTION

If we felt it practical to split hairs or draw lines, we could easily say that this rung of the ladder, which we call action, should be down where rung number two, self-confidence, now is. But our aim is not to draw fine lines. We merely wish to show you how essential all of these rungs are, and point out to you the exact method through which you can develop all of these qualities, thus completing your own magic ladder so it will support you in your upward climb toward your chief aim in life.

We need not argue the point that if there is no action, all the education in the world, all the knowledge that ever came from the best colleges and universities on earth, and all the good intentions plus all the other qualities mentioned in this magic ladder, will not be of any value whatsoever.

The world pays for only one thing, and that is for service rendered, or action. Stored away knowledge is worthless. It benefits no one until it has been expressed in terms of action. No one pays for goods on the shelves; they must be hauled down and ushered into service before the world pays for them.

You might be a graduate of Yale, Harvard, or Princeton; in fact, you might have all the facts in all of the encyclopedias in the world stored away in your head, but unless you organize this knowledge and express it in action, it would be worth nothing to you or to the world.

How many millions of people are there in this world who have all the essentials for great success, who have everything necessary with which to render the world a great service, except one quality: action.

Did the world ever give any person a chance other than that which they went out and created by the use of their imagination, self-confidence, initiative, and those other qualifies mentioned in this ladder?

We need not argue the point that if there is no action. All the education in the world, all the knowledge that ever came from the best colleges and universities on earth, and all the good intentions plus all of the other qualities mentioned in this magic ladder will not be of any value whatsoever.

A person without this great quality of action resembles a great locomotive which stands on the sidetrack or in the round house with coal in the bunker, water in the tank, fire in the firebox, steam in the dome, but no engineer to open the throttle.

This great piece of locomotive power is as useless as a sand dune until someone opens the throttle and puts the thing into action.

Within that head of yours is a great machine, one that rivals all the locomotives and man-made machines every built; but it is as useless as the locomotive which stands on the side of the track without the engineer, until you put it into action.

How many millions of people are there in this world who have all the essentials for great success, who have everything necessary with which to render the world a great service, except one quality: action.

Action is one of the chief qualities which all leaders must possess, and, incidentally, it is the chief quality which distinguishes the leader from those who follow. This is worth thinking about; it may help some of us advance from the rank and file of the followers into the select, limited class who are leaders.

With but little use of your imagination, you can see how closely related action is to all of the other qualities covered by the first four rungs in the ladder. You can see how the lack of action would nullify all of the other qualities. When a person goes into action, those negative qualities of procrastination, fear, worry, and doubt are strictly on the defensive, and nearly everyone knows that a better fight can be fought on the offensive than can be fought on the defensive.

Action is one of the chief qualities which all leaders must possess, and, incidentally, it is the chief qualify which distinguishes the leader from those who follow. This is worth thinking about; it may help some of us advance from the rank and file of the followers into the select, limited class who are leaders.

RUNG 6: ENTHUSIASM

The next rung in the ladder is very appropriately called enthusiasm because enthusiasm usually arouses one to action, therefore, should be closely associated with it in the ladder.

If we were considering the steps of this ladder in the order of their importance, probably enthusiasm would precede action, because there is not apt to be very much action in a person unless there is enthusiasm.

The radiant smile on your face speaks in terms louder than word.
It says, "Stand aside and let me pass! I am a success."

Enthusiasm usually develops automatically when one finds the work for which he or she is best fitted, the work which one likes best. It is not likely that you will be able to maintain very much enthusiasm over work that you dislike; therefore, it behooves you to search diligently until you find the work into which you can throw your whole heart and soul, the work in which you can earnestly and persistently "lose" yourself.

RUNG 7: SELF-CONTROL

For 18 long, perilous years, an arch enemy stood between me and the attainment of my definite aim.

That enemy was lack of self-control.

I was always looking for controversy and argument. Usually, I found it. Most of my time was spent in showing someone that they were wrong, whereas I should have been devoting this valuable time to showing myself that I was wrong.

Finding fault with people is undoubtedly the most unprofitable business one ever engaged in. It makes enemies and demoralizes the spirit of friendship. In no way does it reform or help another person.

Lack of self-control leads to fault finding.

No person ever became a great leader of other people until they first learned to *lead* themselves, through self-control. Self-mastery is the first stepping stone to real achievement, all of which is merely a preachment and does not give the real reason why self-control is an absolutely necessary quality for all who attain real success.

When a person "loses their temper," something takes place in their brain which ought to be understood more generally. An angry person does not really "lose" their temper; they merely inflame it and causes it to draw to their brain those chemicals which, when combined through anger, form a deadly poison. An angry person will throw off enough poison with every exhalation of breath to kill a guinea pig!

There are only three ways of getting rid of poison manufactured by the brain, in anger. One is through the pores of the skin, one is through the lungs, the poison being carried away on the breath in the form of gases, and the other is through the liver, which separates the waste matter from the blood.

When these three roadways become overworked, the surplus poison being manufactured by an angry person is distributed through the system and poisons it, just as would be done if any other deadly and poisonous drug were injected into the blood with the use of a hypodermic syringe.

Anger, hatred, cynicism, pessimism, and other negative states of mind tend to poison the system and should be avoided. They are all a part of that deadly negative called lack of self-control.

RUNG 8: EXCEEDING EXPECTATIONS

I do not believe it possible for anyone to rise above mediocrity without developing this habit of performing more service and better service than is actually paid for in dollars and cents.

The person who makes it a habit to do this is usually regarded as a leader, and without exception, as far as we have any knowledge on the subject, all such people have risen to the top in their profession or business, regardless of other handicaps which may have stood in the way.

A person who renders this sort of service is sure to attract the attention of people who will start a lively competition for their services. No one ever heard of competition over the services of the person who performs as little work as possible to get by with, and who performs that work in a careless manner, in an unwilling spirit.

One reason why the person who performs more service than they are paid for is always in demand is the fact that they meet with so little competition in this practice.

All of the ability on earth, all of the knowledge recorded in all of the books down the ages, all the schooling on earth, will not create a profitable market for the services of a person who renders as little service as possible and makes the quality as poor as will pass. On the other hand, the spirit of willingly performing more work and better work than one is paid to perform is sure to bring its just reward. It will offset many other negative qualities and the lack of many other desirable qualities.

RUNG 9: ATTRACTIVE PERSONALITY

You can readily see that even though you possessed all of the qualities thus far outlined, you would, nevertheless, be very apt to fail in your life work if you did not attract people to you through a pleasing personality.

Personality cannot be defined in one word because it is the sum total of those qualities which distinguish you from every other person on earth. The clothes you wear form a part of your personality, a very important part at that. Your facial expression, as shown by the lines on your face or the lack of these, forms a part of your personality. The words you speak form a very important part of your personality, and mark you instantly, once you have spoken, as a person of refinement or the opposite. Your voice constitutes an important part of your personality, a part which, to be pleasing, must be cultivated, trained, and developed so it is harmonious, rich, and expressed with rhythm. The manner in which you shake hands forms an important part of your personality; therefore, make your handshake firm and vibrant. If you merely permit the other person to shake your limp, cold, lifeless hand, you are displaying that which constitutes a negative personality.

A welcoming personality may be described as one that draws people to you and causes them to find companionship and harmony in your company, while an unattractive personality is one that causes people to want to get as far away from you as possible.

You undoubtedly can analyze yourself and determine whether or not people are attracted to you, and if they are not, you surely can find the reason why. Also, it may be of interest to you to know that the kind of people which you attract to you clearly indicates your own character and personality, because you will attract only those who are in harmony with you and whose characters and nature correspond to that of your own.

An attractive personality usually may be found in the person who:

- speaks gently and kindly, selecting words which do not offend;
- is unselfish and willing to serve others;
- is a friend of all humanity, regardless of politics, religion, creed, or economic viewpoints;
- refrains from speaking unkindly of others, either with or without cause;
- manages to converse without being drawn into an argument or trying to draw others into argument on such debatable subjects as religion and politics;
- sees the good there is in people and overlooks the bad;
- seeks neither to reform nor reprimand others;
- smiles frequently and deeply;
- loves little children, flowers, birds, the growing grass, the trees, and the running brooks;
- sympathizes with all who are in trouble;
- forgives acts of unkindness;
- willingly grants to others the rights to do as they please as long as no one else's rights are interfered with;
- earnestly strives to be constructive in every thought and act;
- encourages others and spurs them on to greater undertakings in some useful work for the good of humanity, by inspiring them with self-confidence;
- is a patient and interested listener and makes a habit of giving the other person a part of the conversation without breaking in and doing all the talking.

If you wish to develop an attractive personality, acquire the art of finding out other people's hobbies and getting them to talk about them.

An attractive personality, like all of the other qualities mentioned in this ladder, is easily developed through the application of applied psychology.

RUNG 10: ACCURATE THOUGHT

After you have learned how to think correctly, you will easily and automatically practice the habit of examining everything that tries to make its way to your mind, to see whether or not it is mere "information" or *facts*! You will learn how to keep away from your mind all of those sense impressions which arise, not from fact, but from prejudices and from hatred, anger, bias, and other false sources.

You will learn how to separate facts into two groups, namely, the relevant and irrelevant or, the important and unimportant. You will learn how to take the "important" facts and organize them, working them into a perfect judgment, or plan of action.

You will learn how to analyze that which you read in magazines and newspapers, making the necessary deductions, reasoning from the known facts to the unknown, and arriving at a well-balanced judgment that is not colored by prejudice or built out of mere "information" that you did not carefully examine.

You will also learn, when you understand how to think correctly, how to put that which others speak orally through the same process, because this will lead you nearer to the truth.

You will learn not to take anything for a fact unless it squares up with your own intelligence, and unless it meets the various tests to which a sound thinker always subjects everything which tries to make its way to his mind.

You will learn, also, not to be influenced by what one person says about another, until you have weighed the statement, examined it, and determined, according to the known principles of correct thinking, whether the statement is false or true.

If scientific thinking will do all of this for you, it is a desirable quality, is it not? It will do all of this, and much more, when you understand the comparatively simple principles through which correct thought is produced.

RUNG 11: CONCENTRATION

Concentration, in the sense that we have made it one of the rungs of this ladder, has reference to the practice of inducing your mind to picture all of the details outlined in your chief aim, or in any undertaking, whether connected with or leading to your chief aim or not, until that picture has been clearly outlined, and practical ways and means of transforming it into reality have been created.

Concentration is the process of causing your imagination to search every crevice and corner of your subconscious mind, wherein is stored away a perfect picture of every sense impression which ever reached your mind through your five senses, and finding all that can be used in connection with the object of the concentration.

Concentration is also the process of bringing together, as electric batteries are connected by wires, the combined strength of all the qualities outlined in this ladder for the purpose of achieving a given end or attaining a given object—the object of the concentration.

It is the process of focusing the powers of thought upon a given subject until the mind has analyzed that subject and separated it into its component parts, then re-assembled it again into a definite plan.

It is the process of studying effects by their causes and, conversely, causes by their effects.

RUNG 12: PERSISTENCE

Persistence and concentration are so closely related that it is hard to say where is the line which separates them.

Persistence is synonymous with willpower or determination. It is the quality which causes you to keep the powers of your mind focused upon a given objective, through the principle of concentration, until that objective has been reached.

Persistence is the quality which causes you to arise, when once you have been knocked down by temporary failure, and continue your pursuit of a given desire or object. It is the quality which gives you courage and faith to keep on trying in the face of any and all obstacles which may confront you.

It is the quality which causes the bulldog to find the death grip on his opponent's throat and then lie down and hold on in spite of all efforts to shake him off.

However, you are not aiming to develop persistence for the purpose of using it as a bulldog does. You are developing it for the purpose of carrying you over those necessary rocks and reefs which nearly every person must master in reaching any worthwhile place in the world. You are developing persistence to guide you unwavering in a given direction only after you are satisfied that you are going in the right direction. Indiscriminate use of persistence might only get you in trouble.

RUNG 13: FAILURES

This brings us to the "lucky" thirteenth rung of the ladder: failures. Do not stumble on this rung!

It is the most interesting rung of all because it deals with facts which you must face in life, whether you wish to do so or not, and shows you, as clearly as you might see the sun on a clear day, how you can turn every failure into an asset, how you can carve every failure into a foundation stone upon which your house of success will stand forever.

Failure is the only subject in the whole ladder which might be called "negative," and we shall show you how and why it is one of the most important of life's experiences.

Failure is nature's plan of hurdle-jumping a person and training him for a worthwhile work in life. It is nature's great crucible and tempering process which burns the dross from all the other human qualities and purifies the metal so it will withstand all hard usage throughout life.

Failure is the great law of resistance which makes a person stronger in proportion to the extent that they overcome this resistance.

In every failure, there is a great and lasting lesson if one will only analyze, think, and profit by it. Failure develops tolerance, sympathy, and kindness in the human heart.

You will not travel very far down life's pathway before you discover that every adversity and every failure is a blessing in disguise, a blessing because it has put your mind and your body into action and, thereby, caused both to grow through the law of use.

Look back down the ages, and you will find history full of incidents which clearly show the cleansing, purifying, strengthening value of failure.

When you begin to realize that failure is a necessary part of one's education, you will no longer look upon it with fear, and the first thing you know, there will be no more failures. No person ever arose from the knockout blow of defeat without being a stronger and wiser human being in one respect or another.

If you will look back over your own failures, if you are fortunate enough to be able to point to any of very great consequence, you will no doubt see that those failures marked certain turning points in your life and in your plans which were of benefit to you.

RUNG 14: TOLERANCE AND SYMPATHY

One of the curses of this world today is intolerance and lack of sympathy. Had the world been tolerant, the World Wars could never have swept the face of the civilized globe as they did.

Here in America, it is of particular importance that we learn the lesson of tolerance and sympathy, for the reason that this is a great melting pot in which we are living side by side with every race, and with the followers of every creed and religion on earth.

Unless we display tolerance and sympathy, we are not living up to the standard which first distinguished this from the old world across the Atlantic.

Many great lessons were learned during wars, but none was of more importance than this: that people of all religions and all nationalities and races could fight side by side for a common cause.

If we could fight for a common cause during war, without displaying intolerance for one another on account of religion, race, and creed, and if we found it necessary and profitable to do so, who not continue to do the same in peace?

Power comes out of cooperation. The masses could lay aside intolerance and work for a common cause, behind a solid front, and no power on earth could defeat them!

In warfare, defeat usually comes from lack of organization. The same is true in life. Intolerance and lack of harmonious effort, to a common end, has always left the door open so that a few who understood the power that comes from organized effort might step right in and ride the back of the disorganized, intolerant masses.

Just now intolerance is working havoc with the world in two directions, namely, in religion and in business and industry. The disagreement between so-called "capital" and "labor" is nothing but intolerance and greed, and it is as much in evidence on one side as it is on the other. If both sides would see that one is the arm while the other is the life-blood which keeps that arm alive, each would see that intolerance which affects one adversely also affects the other in the same way.

Let us be done with intolerance by placing *principle* above the dollar and *humanity* above the selfish individual. Let us exercise at least as much real intelligence as does the little honeybee that works for the good of the hive, that the hive may not perish.

RUNG 15: WORK

This is the shortest word of all those which constitute the rungs of his ladder, yet it is one of the most important of those qualities.

All of nature's laws have decreed that nothing may live which is not used. The arm which is tied to one's side and removed from active use will wither up and perish away. So it is with any other part of the physical body. Disuse brings decay and death.

Likewise, the human mind, with all of its qualities, will wither up and decay unless it is used. This is wrong. The mind will not decay, but the brain, the physical agent through which the mind functions, will decay unless it is used.

Every picture which reaches the human brain, through the five senses, imbeds itself upon one of the tiny brain cells, there to wither up and die through disuse, or to become vivid and healthy, through constant use.

The most modern educators now concede that it is not the actual knowledge which a child gathers from schoolbooks which constitutes their "education." It is the brain development which takes place in the process of transferring that knowledge from the books to the brain, bringing a corresponding amount of use of the brain itself, which constitutes the real value of schooling.

The qualities outlined in this ladder are yours in return for just one price, and that price is work—persistent, never-ceasing work. As long as you exercise these qualities and keep them at work, they will be strong and healthy. But if you permit them to lie dormant, unused, they will wither into decay and finally into death.

RUNG 16: THE GOLDEN RULE

This is the last rung of the ladder, yet but slight reflection will tell us that it probably should have been the first rung, because its use or disuse will determine whether one ultimately fails or succeeds in the application of all the other qualities mentioned in the ladder.

The Golden Rule philosophy is the shining sun which should form the background of all the other qualities outlined in the ladder. Unless the Golden Rule lights the pathway over which you travel, you are apt to plunge headlong into pitfalls from which you can never escape.

The Golden Rule philosophy makes Kaisers impossible and helps to produce Lincolns and Washingtons. It is the thing which leads individuals or nations into growth or decay, life or death, according to whether it is applied or not.

The Golden Rule acts as a barrier to all of man's tendencies toward the destructive use of the power which comes from developing the other qualities outlined in this ladder. It is the thing which antidotes the harm people could do without knowledge and power, the thing which guides people to the intelligent, constructive use of those qualities which they develop from the use of the rungs of this ladder.

The Golden Rule is the torch light by which a person is guided toward those objectives in life which leave something of value to posterity, which lightens the burdens of their fellow sojourners on earth and helps them find the way to useful, constructive effort.

The Golden Rule simply means that we must act toward others as we wish others to act toward us; that we must do unto them as we wish to be done unto us; that we must give thoughts, actions, and deeds which we are willing to receive from others.

You have before you, in this ladder, a perfect blueprint or plan by which you can reach any legitimate undertaking in life which is within possible reach of a person of your age, natural tendency, schooling, and environment. The ladder is a mental ladder to guide you to look for the end of the rainbow of success which nearly all of us expect to find at some point in life.

Your rainbow's end is in sight, my friend, and the moment you master the qualities in this ladder, you can pick up the bag of gold which is waiting there for the rightful owner to come along and claim it.

⚡ ENTREPRENEUR ACTION ITEM
Become the Best Version of Yourself

Hill's Success Ladder is legendary. You'd be hard-pressed to find any quality or habit-based philosophy for business (and life!) that doesn't speak to the rungs he mentions in this essay. A big takeaway from this piece is that living an authentic life is a multifaceted effort. You have to put in the work to get the reward—the best version of you that you can share with not only your friends and family but also with your colleagues and contemporaries.

To be powerful in the business world you must possess the essential qualities that will guarantee to keep you ahead of the game. The majority of people do not reach the levels of success or satisfaction they desire, not because they don't have the talent, but because they do not have the other qualities necessary to make it happen. To live as powerfully as you desire, you must embody the indispensable qualities of those who have reached the mecca of success before you. Here are some more rungs you might want to add to your own personal ladder of success:

Live Fiercely

Living fiercely means you challenge yourself to live life to the fullest. Do not compare yourself to others. Your only real competition is with your own self-doubt. If you cater to your doubt, it will partner with "delay" and you will struggle to initiate and follow through. You may live an average life, but it won't be a satisfying life. Living fiercely means you go at life with your whole heart. The more fiercely you live, the more wonderful life becomes. Those who have succeeded, those who have the wealth and happiness you desire, have lived fiercely.

Care Deeply

Caring deeply means you know who you are, what you need and how to have compassion for yourself. In doing this, you increase your capacity to care for all others; even those whom you would prefer not to spend time with. If you cannot be kind, you must have the grace to remain silent. Further, when you care deeply about what you do, what your purpose is, and the effort and quality of the work you put into yourself, your passions, and others, it will show. Caring deeply helps you create sustainable networks that are supportive of your efforts. Caring deeply is contagious, as it inspires others to want to be a part of what you're doing.

Accept Reality

Unforgivable things are going to happen. You will face plenty of loss and betrayal. To protect your success, you must accept the reality of the people and circumstances which have been set for your destruction. Acceptance brings you to reality and reality is the only place you can start to heal from in an effort to change your life. Reality is where forgiveness and wisdom combine. To be successful, you must learn to "drop it, leave it, and let it go." Forgiveness is an essential ingredient when it comes to success, whereas, your wisdom lies in not forgetting. When you remember who and what did not have your best interest at heart, you are less likely to make those mistakes again in the future.

Be Discerning

You cannot host toxic people and rise in your life or career at the same time. For this reason, to be as successful and fulfilled as you desire, you must be discerning about the company you keep. You cannot fly with bowling balls attached to your wings. For this reason, rid your path of toxic people as soon as you recognize their toxicity. It only takes one toxic person to destroy the progress of many. Success is about surrounding yourself with a team of people who are similar in drive, variable in skills, and driven from the same infectious passion that motivates you. The key to your success, will always stem from the quality of your personal relationships.

Stay Positive

To live an empowered life, you must train your mindset to believe in your capacity to succeed. You must choose to carry a mental and emotional attitude focused on the bright side of life. Empowerment is ultimately a state of consciousness where you anticipate happiness, health, success, and the belief that you can overcome any obstacle or difficulty. Say Yes to life, to new opportunities, thoughts, ideas, and directions. You must allow your mind to be open, flexible and to trust that each time you say yes, that you will be led into more success.

Have Grit

Trust that failure is the springboard for your success. Each mistake made is designed to take you in a new direction, rather than designed to take you down. You must refuse to allow setbacks to discourage you. Let setbacks inspire you more deeply to set new goals, to generate new ideas and to take novel ways up the mountain. Let there be no amount of hard work you will shy away from, regardless of how talented you are. Hold the awareness that having a talent for something is far different than excelling at something; therefore, your hard work will trump your talent every time. To feel empowered on any level, you must have the grit to finish what you start.

Stay Humble

To live from a state of empowerment, you must have the humility to know when you need to ask for help, and when it is time to allow the efforts of others to shine more brightly than your own. Humility gives you the wisdom to understand that success is a shared experience. When achievements can be shared, it makes you more engaging to others, as your humility naturally draws intrigue. There is nothing more beautiful than to give credit to the team of people who helped you get to where you are.

Set Boundaries

As important as it is to say yes, you must also know when to say no. Overextending yourself to an oppressive schedule that doesn't allow you to take care of your health, nutrition, to get adequate sleep or enough time for your personal life is not success at all, it's slavery. Success is not empowering if you do not have your health, the experience of deep love and the time to live your life wholeheartedly. It is crucial to take breaks from the grind, and to experience the fruits of your labor. If you say no to one opportunity, another will come along that will be even better. Say no whenever necessary to establish a healthy work/life balance.

Be Courageous

The motto you must live by, is to *feel the fear and do it anyway.* To experience empowerment, you have to put guts over fear. You must face your fears if you want to know what you're capable of. How can you know the depth of your capacity if you never test it? You've got this one life, so you may as well test the limits of what you believe your capacities to be, and prove your more limiting beliefs to be false. To be in the game of success, you've got to be in it to win it.

Be Tough-Minded

You must not allow giving up to be a viable option. If you're seeking to live your dream, you are the only person who can go out there and live it. You cannot give up in the middle of the race just because the finish line isn't coming fast enough. Stay in the moment, learn patience, and keep working hard. Your hard work and tough-mindedness will give you a resilience to outlast your competitors. Most people are not tough-minded enough to be patient or to tolerate uncertainty; they want the quick-fix and the easy win. If you want to live an empowered life, you must become a warrior, skilled in the area of perseverance. You must view each challenge as a competition to be won.

CHAPTER EIGHT

The Power of Organized Effort

This article is based upon scientific facts. If you analyze it carefully, you will find out what the fundamentals are which mark the difference between a LEADER and a FOLLOWER. It clearly shows how power is attained.

To prepare you for that which is to follow, let me outline a few simple similes. To begin with, let us consider liberated steam such as we have seen floating in the air after a passing train has disappeared.

Such steam is without power.

But a few minutes previously, it had sufficient power to pull the train, but that was while it was concentrated, confined, or organized!

There is no power in a flowing river as long as the water is spread out from bank to bank, but concentrate that same water into a mill race, by organizing it and diverting its course, through the aid of a dam, and it will turn the wheels of industry.

Out of organized effort comes power.

An ordinary change of gunpowder is practically harmless when exploded in the open air, but confine the same amount of powder and control its energy through the aid of a gun barrel, and it becomes dynamic and powerful.

The sun's rays will not burn a hole in a newspaper, even on the hottest day, unless they are organized and concentrated on that paper through the aid of a reading glass; but the organization through the aid of the glass gives the rays power to burn a hole in the paper instantly.

With this preparation, we are ready to discuss the subject of this article, which is man-power and how it is attained. Man-power is developed, just like all other power, through organized effort. This organization takes on two forms. One is the organization of one's own faculties, and the other is the organization of people into groups. A highly organized group of highly organized individuals can accomplish startling results.

History is full of evidence that a small army of well-trained, well-organized soldiers have defeated ten times their number of disorganized, poorly trained soldiers.

And, here is a thought which is meant for you. Be sure to appropriate it to your own use, and you can attain to whatever heights you may aspire to reach. It is this:

A well-organized individual can carry out their plans in spite of the opposition of those around them. A single individual can so thoroughly organize their knowledge, their facts, and their plans that the whole human race cannot stop them from accomplishing whatever they may undertake.

All of which is in the nature of a prelude to what we wish to say on the subject of organized effort.

Let us turn to the subject of showing you how to organize your individual faculties to the end that you may gain man-power.

Generally speaking there are two classes of people in the world, and we must take this into consideration before we can get a proper perspective of this subject of organized effort about which I am writing. These two classes of people are leaders and followers. The two classes are very unevenly divided. Ninety-five percent of the adult population of the world are followers, and the other 5 percent are leaders.

The chief difference between the two is that one class have organized themselves and learned how to organize those around them, while the other class is unorganized, both as individuals and as a group of people.

You will observe, therefore, that there are two kinds of organization. One is individual organization, and the other is group organization.

Let's begin with the individual, and let's call that individual you.

You can transform yourself into a regular human dynamo of power and leadership if you will observe these suggestions and apply them to the end that you may organize your faculties. First, you must cultivate the 16 qualities outlined in the Magic Ladder to Success [which you read about in the previous chapter]. You must understand and apply every one of these 16 principles, the first one of which is a "definite aim in life." Going on up the ladder, you must develop:

- self-confidence
- initiative
- imagination
- action
- enthusiasm
- self-control
- the habit of performing more service than you are paid for
- an attractive personality
- the ability to think accurately and concentrate all your efforts on a single goal
- persistency

You must also:

- learn to profit by all your failures and mistakes, taking and applying the lesson that each brings you;
- cultivate tolerance and sympathy;
- find the work for which you are best suited, the work which you like best;
- base all of your human relationships on the Golden Rule philosophy.

This will start you in the right direction in organizing your individual faculties into power. To the degree that you fail to master and apply any of the 16 principles of the magic ladder to success, will you lack the power that comes from organized effort. After you have thoroughly organized yourself, you will be ready to step out of that overwhelmingly large crowd called followers, if you are now in that crowd, and take your place among the leaders.

In no other way can you attain to leadership.

Unless you organized your faculties according to the formula laid down in the magic ladder to success, you might as well content yourself to remain a follower, a member of that large human family called "wage-bound." You will have to submit to injustice and to the rulership of others, whether you want to do so or not, unless you organize yourself into a unit of man-power that will enable you to throw off the yoke of oppression and rise to where you wish to be in life.

There is no escape from poverty, grief, sorrow, and injustice save through organized effort.

Please read the foregoing paragraph again, and if in reading it a second time, you will ponder its meaning, get its significance, and apply the thought that comes from it, you can rise to the heights of human attainment in a matter of weeks or months.

It may seem unjust for one person to live with comparative ease, without the use of his hands, without making any strenuous effort, but regardless of what it may seem, there is only one way for you to avoid such seeming injustice, and that is by organizing your faculties and creating the power that will enable you to throw off the burdens that have been fastened on you.

Remember, I am not indulging in a preachment. Leadership and individual power come from organized effort, and organized effort comes from organizing the individual faculties, then by directing these faculties to a definite end, through definite plans.

Get this principle clearly fixed in your mind, and you will understand how futile and useless it is to curse and rail at your "unlucky" lot in life. You can change your "luck" only by organizing your efforts, by understanding cause and effect.

If you want to know why one person can become a millionaire while their neighbor, who is just as deserving morally, or perhaps more so, remains a pauper, I can tell you: One has the ability to organize and intelligently direct their efforts according to a definite plan, and the other does not have this ability. Perhaps a better way to state it is that one has developed and organized their faculties into organized effort, while the other, through lack of understanding or out of lethargic passivity toward life, has failed to organize theirs.

In closing, I would leave with you this thought: Who is there to stop you from thoroughly organizing yourself and climbing to the heights in any undertaking which you may choose? Who is there with power enough to stop you, if they chose to do so, if you organized your faculties and directed your efforts to a definite end, in an organized manner? If you belong to that great mass called "wage-bound," who must be at a certain place at a certain hour, every day of their lives, in order to get the necessary food and clothing for existence, who is there to stop you from organizing your faculties to such an extent that you can eventually take a day off, at least?

Answer these questions. The answer may lead you out of the wilderness of poverty and failure into the light of success and plenty. Who knows without trying!

⸢ ENTREPRENEUR ACTION ITEM
Organize Your Day

Disorganization is costly. Whether you're at home or in the office, it's stressful to be always looking for something. Organized people don't have that stress. Studies have found that reducing clutter eliminates 40 percent of housework in the average home. The average office employee spends over an hour each day looking for things. Nearly one-in-four adults (23 percent) say they're late paying their bills just because they lose them.

The good news? You don't have to be another statistic. You can become much more organized by following these five tactics of well-organized people.

Set Morning and Evening Rituals

Morning and evening rituals keep you from stumbling around mindlessly throughout the day. As a result, you'll be more productive and successful. The daily rituals that organized people practice include:

_/_ Waking up before everyone else to prepare their day without being pulled into a million different directions.

_/_ Not checking their phone immediately to avoid getting lost in emails and social media.

_/_ Doing something they enjoy, such as reading a book or meditating, to clear their minds.

_/_ Completing tasks in the same order. For example, they brush their teeth, then take a shower.

_/_ Identifying three things for a successful day. Think through your day first thing in the morning. Decide what three top tasks you can complete to make you feel like the day was a success, then schedule them.

_/_ Setting realistic learning goals. They just add one thing at a time. They also limit the number of tasks that need to be completed.

_/_ Preparing the night before. Regardless if it's lunch, their wardrobe, or a presentation, planning out their day the night before prevents scuttling around.

_/_ Tweaking their to-do-lists. To-do-lists are started the night before and are adjusted in the morning if new priorities developed overnight.

_/_ They "eat the frog." They complete the task that they don't want to do first thing in morning. This allows them to have a productive day since it's not weighing them down.

_/_ De-clutter. Before leaving for work they make sure the house is clean so they can come home and relax. They also tidy up their workplace at the end of the day. Doing so ensures that they won't waste time looking for misplaced items.

Clear Your Brain

Get your thoughts out of your head and onto paper. Organized individuals keep to-do lists, for example, in one spot so they won't forget anything. They don't spread their lists across notepads, Post-Its or tablet. As an added perk, this also reduces anxiety.

Once everything has been written down on a list, you want to divide it into four categories. According to David Allen's _Getting Things Done_ (Penguin, 2002) these categories are: "Do it, Delegate it, Defer it, and Drop it."

What that means to you is that by following this organized way of tackling your to-do list, you won't get in a feedback loop of trying to decide how to complete the task. Best to just get it out in the universe (on paper), make a decision about execution, then do it and move on.

Research shows that when things are left unfinished we worry. The solution? Write everything down.

Downsize

Why spend the time and energy organizing possessions that you no longer need or want? Organized individuals set aside the time to periodically purge. Tossing clothing that no longer fits you or notes from completed tasks prevents clutter from building up over.

But, this isn't just a one-time occurrence. Organized individuals constantly evaluate their belongings. If it's no longer working for them they ditch it. This avoids marathon purging sessions since they de-clutter in small doses.

Use Tools

Anything from kitchen timers, time tracking tools, apps like Evernote, and multipurpose furniture are used by those who are organized. They use these items for reminders, to visualize time more effectively and remain on-track.

For example, Evernote and other timesaving tools can keep thoughts and information in one location. Bookshelves can be used to zone out rooms while creating a dedicated place for your belongings.

Reject Perfectionism

Not all organized people are perfectionists—and you shouldn't be, either. Nicole Anzia, owner of Neatnik, writes in the *Washington Post*, "Most organized people realize they can't possibly do everything perfectly and get everything done. They prioritize tasks and learn where and how to take shortcuts and how to complete tasks quickly."

"They don't get mired in projects that will be impossible to finish on time. In other words, they don't let perfection get in the way of progress."

CHAPTER NINE

The Master Mind

Through organized effort comes power. If you would attain financial success, you must get a firm hold on this principle of organized, cooperative effort.

Fourteen years ago, Andrew Carnegie made a statement which I did not hear until 10 years later.

During a newspaper interview with the great steel magnate, I asked him to what he attributed his success. He replied by asking me to define the term *success*. When I told him I had reference to his money, he said:

"Well, if you want to know how I got my money, I will refer you to these men here on my staff; they got it for me. We have here in this business a master mind. It is not my mind, and it is not the mind of any other man on my staff, but the sum total of all these minds that I have gathered around me that constitute a master mind in the steel business. I have been many years gathering these men around me and building this mind. Each man contributes an important part to the building of this mind. I do not always agree with all the men on my staff, on all matters, nor do they always agree with me; perhaps some of us do not like each other from a personal viewpoint, but I know that I need these men, and they know that they need me in the maintenance of this master mind which is necessary in carrying on this steel business."

For years afterward, I wondered just what Carnegie meant by "master mind." In the light of more mature years, it began to dawn upon me that he had stated a whole life's philosophy in a few words. Carnegie knew the value of organized effort. He knew that no one person could accomplish very much without the coordinated effort of other minds. He knew the value of cooperation. He had on his staff people who did not always agree with him. He had people whom he did not always admire in every respect and who, perhaps, did not always admire him, but each knew that they needed the others; therefore, they harmonized their efforts toward a common end with the result that all profited.

I wonder if there is not a great lesson for the remainder of us in the history of Carnegie's accumulation of one of the greatest fortunes this country has ever seen. I wonder if his plan of making use of organized effort could not be applied to all walks of life. Following in Carnegie's footsteps, and making use of exactly the same philosophy, Mr. Chas. M. Schwab is rapidly duplicating Carnegie's success. Is it not possible for anyone else to apply the same principle in any legitimate business undertaking with equal success?

What a remarkable strength is shown by a person who can lay aside personal prejudices and work without friction with a group of people with whom they are not in accord on many subjects. What remarkable genius it shows when a person can exercise sufficient self-control, as did Carnegie and as Mr. Schwab is now doing, in working side-by-side with people of different racial and religious viewpoints, with never a thought of friction, with never a sign of intolerance. I would give considerably if I could purchase from Mr. Schwab the privilege of working with him for a few months for the purpose of studying his simple procedure in applying this principle of organized effort which has raised him from the work of humble coachman to the head of one of America's greatest industries, employing thousands of people.

Out of organized effort comes power, and the process of organization begins, always, in the mind of some one person who organizes the faculties of his own mind and then gathers other minds around him and teaches them how to organize themselves and how to do teamwork. Oh to be such a genius, with the self-control and the spirit of tolerance to work with others toward a definite goal, without selfishness or haughtiness.

ENTREPRENEUR ACTION ITEM
Build and Manage Your Team Using Emotional Intelligence

What Hill describes in the piece above is a "team of rivals" approach to leadership. By letting go of your assumptions and preconceived biases about others, you can build a stronger team that plays to the strengths of each member. Focusing on what unique benefits each team member brings to the table and allowing each person to use those skills to reach your common goal isn't always easy, but by practicing a more mindful approach to hiring and management helps. Sharpening your emotional intelligence (EQ) skills is one way to clear your path to doing this.

The World Economic Forum has named emotional intelligence as one of the top skills needed for success in 2020. But what is it? Too often, people reduce emotional intelligence to "emotional awareness," or the knowledge that cues you into your feelings. "I am happy; I am sad; I am frustrated."

Yet emotional self-awareness is but one very small part of the whole. Emotional intelligence is comprised of five parts: self-perception, self-expression, interpersonal, decision making, and stress management. Therefore, emotional intelligence as a whole could be defined as the ability to know yourself and perceive your emotions, express yourself assertively and independently, have mutually satisfying relationships with others, make decisions from a grounded, secure place, and manage stress well while facing the future with optimism.

An emotionally intelligent person is someone who lives—and works—well.

As a leader within your organization, you should make it your goal to evolve the company's EQ. Emotionally intelligent teams are healthier and more productive. They communicate better, work toward goals with enthusiasm and focus, and have stronger relationships among teammates. Thus, your company succeeds and employee retention soars.

How healthy is your company's EQ? Here are some signs that it may be time to uplevel emotional intelligence:

l High turnover rate

l Stress-induced sickness prevalent in the workplace

l Culture of backbiting and gossip

l Communication gaps between managers and direct reports

l Mistakes are severely punished

l Select few employees are preferred, while the rest are largely forgotten

l Personal and professional development is not taken seriously

l Workplace is not inclusive of employees from diverse backgrounds

Emotional intelligence starts at the top. That means if either of these "warning signs" are prevalent in your workplace, it's incumbent on leadership to create a healthier, more kind environment in which team members can do their best work.

It's not enough to succeed by hitting sales goals, or discovering an elusive algorithm, or landing the biggest client. Your success as an organizational leader is directly tied to the health and success of those who report to you. There's the old saying, "If you want to go fast, go alone; if you want to go far, go together."

How successful can you be if a flood of employees leaves every month because they feel that their managers browbeat them? Or if your C-Suite works such long hours that exhaustion-induced hospital check-ins are not unheard of? Or if you've failed to hire diverse candidates for the last five years, and now you are lacking key perspectives and are falling behind the competition?

As a leader, the best thing you can do for your company is to prioritize upleveling your emotional intelligence. This won't benefit just your work, by the way. Since "upleveling your emotional intelligence" could be called "becoming a healthily-functioning human," *all* your relationships will benefit from taking your EQ to the next level.

Improved EQ can allow co-workers to have truthful conversations with each other for the first time in years. People can stop shifting blame onto others and own their part in any dysfunction occurring in the workplace—and hence, see their way forward to the solution. EQ can help leaders face head-on the challenges coming toward them via a changing marketplace, and create an informed, grounded plan as to how they'll adapt. It can do the same for you.

CHAPTER TEN

Some Interesting Facts Concerning Character Analysis

This is the first of a series of articles on the interesting subject of character analysis. This article is based upon actual facts gathered and classified from the analysis of over 10,000 people, representing nearly every calling, in all walks of life.

A young man stepped into my office five years ago and asked abruptly, "What can you do for a down-and-outer?"

I handed him an analysis chart and seated him at a desk with instructions to fill it out carefully, then turned to interview my next visitor. Ordinarily, the time required in which to properly fill out the personal analysis chart which I use will average about 30 minutes.

In fifteen minutes, the young man was back at my desk with the chart neatly filled out.

I took the chart, folded it without looking at it, laid it on the desk before me, extended my hand to the young man before me, and I said to him, "I want to congratulate you on account of your unusual ability to concentrate your mind on whatever you are doing until it has been finished. I also want to congratulate you on account of your unusual enthusiasm.

"With these two qualities as well developed as they are in you, I feel that my task in analyzing you and starting you on the road to success is a comparatively easy one."

The young man blushed, stammered something about being "down on his luck," and started to tell me why he had never been able to advance in any position, but I stopped him. I saw, as clearly as I might have seen the sun on a bright day, the reason why, in spite of the fact that I had not unfolded his personal analysis chart.

I turned to the chart and began to read the subtle story which he told, every paragraph, every line, and every word of which corroborated the story which I had already read from the few remarks he made when he came into the office.

This young man was an interesting case because he is typical of that class, running into the hundreds of thousands, who go through life dismal failures, largely on account of one shortcoming, a shortcoming which can be eliminated in 999 out of every 1,000 cases.

Let me give you a brief resume of what that personal analysis chart disclosed.

First of all, it disclosed the fact that the young man had a splendid schooling, including three years of college work and a special course in a leading university. It also disclosed the fact that he had a quick, apt brain, that he had the ability to analyze correctly, that he was far above the average as a thinker; that he had an unusually attractive personality, that he was not afraid of work.

In fact, he had all the essential qualities for success except one, and that was self-confidence!

Before I was halfway through analyzing him, I asked him this question: "If you were offered a position as principal of a high school at $3,000 a year, would you accept it?" He hesitated, turned his head from side to side for a few moments, and then started to say something, but I stopped him with, "Thanks. I thought not!"

He protested that he had not given me his answer yet, but I begged leave to inform him that he had—he answered me when he hesitated.

He then insisted on stating his case in these words:

"Now, it is like this: If I could hold the job, I would accept it, but I never earned as much as $3,000 a year, and I, therefore, doubt that I could hold down that sort of a job."

I closed my eyes for a moment and looked back into the dim past. I saw myself in the place of the young man before me. I knew exactly how he felt, and why he felt that way.

I went ahead with his analysis until I completed it and formulated my plan for shaking him out of the rut into which he had drifted.

The completed analysis showed just two points of contact at which I had to take hold of that young man—just two weaknesses—but these two were the most dangerous of the score or more which beset the pathway of the average person who fails to get ahead in life.

These two weaknesses were lack of self-confidence, as I have already stated, and lack of a definite purpose in life.

My work, heretofore, was reduced, by the process of elimination, to the task of helping the young man find the particular kind of work for which he was best fitted by temperament, physical build, training, and natural inclination, and to helping him develop the self-confidence necessary to pursue that work to success.

I have selected this particular case because it represents nearly seventy-five percent of all whom I analyze, and about the same percentage of the 10,000 people whom I have analyzed in the past.

We want to hear the truth about ourselves, but woe be unto the one who hands it to us without a sugar coating.

All salespeople will do well to remember that no one wants anything that someone else is trying to get "rid" of.

If you must keep your troubles alive, plant them—plant them under six feet of soil and be careful to forget the burying place.

STARTING ON THE ROAD TO SUCCESS

I began first the task of finding the life work in which he would enjoy his greatest success, a matter quite easily determined in 99 out of a 100 cases.

The process through which this data is secured automatically reduced the possible lines of work to three, one of which was a line of work in which the young man had had no experience whatsoever. The other two lines he had tried without success.

By applying the test which I use in cases of this kind, I decided to try the young man out in the work in which he had had no experience.

When I made known to him my decision, he said, "I always did wish to might engage in that sort of work, but I never believed I could do it."

Those words relieved me, to a large extent, of the work I would have had to do in preparing him for the work that I had selected, because they told me in no uncertain terms that the young man would automatically help in developing self-confidence because I had prescribed work into which he could throw his whole heart and soul.

This brings me to a suitable place at which to say that one of the most interesting things I have learned from character analysis is the fact that a person will succeed in a big way, 99 times out of a 100, when properly analyzed, classified, and given work into which they can throw their whole heart and soul.

I look upon this work of analyzing character and fitting people to jobs as being more than an economic issue; it helps people find the greatest thing in life: happiness!

If viewed from a business standpoint, the work is not profitable, but if viewed from the standpoint of service rendered to one's fellow humans who need it, and the happiness which comes from such service, its value is priceless.

I believe it a conservative statement when I say that success can be guaranteed in one hundred percent of the cases where a person can be properly guided in the selection and pursuit of a definite purpose of life (providing, of course, that this purpose places his or her in the work for which best fitted), and sufficient self-confidence can be developed with which to pursue that purpose to a finish.

/ ENTREPRENEUR TIP

Need to boost your self-esteem? Talk yourself into it! Take a few moments each morning to do a little positive self-talk. Think of three things you really like about yourself, then try to notice those in action as you move through your day.

I cannot recall a single client whom I have served in whom immediate and satisfactory results were not noticeable, excepting those in whom self-confidence could not be developed (which are a negligible number), and those who could not be persuaded to follow the work for which they were best fitted.

Some people are so negatively lacking in self-confidence and in ability to concentrate their attention on one line of work that success is impossible.

NEGATIVE QUALITIES THAT STAND BETWEEN PEOPLE AND SUCCESS

I began the analysis of people over ten years ago, as part of my research work in the field of psychology. At that time, I had no notion of serving professionally in the field of character analysis. The information disclosed, as I began to classify and record the common weaknesses of thousands of people, readily told me that this is one of the greatest fields of human endeavor, a field in which a great service can be rendered to humanity. Incidentally, the startling facts disclosed in this analysis work have played an important part in my own life, and have laid the foundation for most of the editorials which I have written.

One of the most startling things I have discovered after I had analyzed and classified the first thousand people, was the fact that 95 percent of them had no definite aim in life. Not one of those who had no definite aim was successful, and but few of them were earning a satisfactory living.

Another startling thing was discovered in connection with this fact, namely, that the majority of those whom I analyzed immediately saw their weakness of not having a definite aim in life, and its effect on their progress, merely by filling out a personal analysis chart.

One woman, of excellent education, cultured and refined, who had found it necessary to drift from one thing to another until she was then doing ordinary house cleaning, exclaimed jubilantly, "That's been my trouble all my life," when she came to the question in the personal analysis chart which reads as follows: "Have you a definite aim in life, and if so, state what it is in detail, when and how you expect to attain it?"

This woman became so enthusiastic over the "new reservoir of thought which that question had developed" in her brain, as she explained it, that she insisted on stopping the analysis right here. She said that there was no use analyzing any further—that she had found her weakness and would promptly eliminate it and return to see me again.

She went away, and I did not hear from her for nearly a year. One day, I received a package from her in which she enclosed some samples of her work. She had engaged as a writer of specialty advertising copy, and those samples of her work readily disclosed the fact that she had selected the right vocation. She is now engaged with one of the largest agencies in the country. I do not know what salary she receives, but she informs me that she soon will have her own home paid for out of her savings from her work. Best of all, she adds this remark:

"And I am happier than I ever thought a person could be. I have found my place in the world, and my work is not work at all; it is play, and I love it."

"And I love it!"

These words told the whole story.

But not all cases are so easily handled as was this woman's, with reference to the selection of a chief aim in life. Most of them have drifted so long that they have not only lost hope of finding the work for which they are best fitted, the work which they love and will follow to the exclusion of all else, but they have also lost or never enjoyed the necessary self-confidence with which to follow the work when discovered.

Another negative quality which I found standing in the way of nearly all whom I analyzed is lack of initiative. They had never seen the importance of doing more than was required of them, or of inviting themselves into leadership now and then.

The personal analysis chart which I use is so arranged that it readily discloses whether or not a person has self-control. The majority of those whom I have analyzed lacked self-control. They allowed themselves to be swayed by their emotions and passions just as a gust of wind would sway blades of grass.

In the entire first thousand people analyzed, I found only one person who exercised enough self-control to enable him to stay with his job in spite of all disagreeable circumstances that might arise from day to day to make him want to quit!

Incidentally, this person is now holding one of the most important jobs with one of the great steel companies. At the time of this analysis, he was working with the same company, as a laborer in the mills.

The chief reason that lack of self-control stands in the way of success is the fact that a person who lacks will "strike back" at every person who offends them, will become angered at every obstacle which places itself in their way, will make remarks that gain them the enmity of their fellow employees and their employers, or the public whom they serve, thereby steadily building a host of enemies which finally make their success impossible.

No person is wanted in any position if they lack the self-control which is essential in attracting people to them and causing others to like them. A person may have every technical quality essential for success in a given field of work, but unless that person curbs their temper and exercises self-control, they are doomed to ultimate failure. This is no mere preachment or hypothesis. I am passing on to you that which was disclosed by actual tests and careful analyses. In fact, the chief value of this article is that it is based upon authentic facts, arrived at by accurate, scientific analysis, and classification in over 10,000 cases.

The world needs a new school of salesmanship that will teach its students to sell sunshine, smiles, and good fellowship along with their goods and wares.

Another disagreeable and destructive tendency of those who lack self-control is that of slandering their fellow humans. My experience in personal analysis work has done more to curb my own tongue than anything that has ever happened, because it has shown me what must be the fate of all who indulge in slandering another person, no matter what the provocation for doing so may be.

I would place my hands on a person afflicted with leprosy just as quickly as I would go into another person's family closet and drag out their family skeleton, or slander them in any way, with or without cause. In one case, physical death would be certain; in the other, a more dreaded death would be just as sure: moral death.

Another startling discovery which I made was the common tendency among people to hate one another on account of difference in religious belief, politics, race, and the like. Lack of tolerance showed itself in nearly every case which I have analyzed, and this had a marked effect in keeping the person in poverty and failure.

THE GREATEST FACTS LEARNED FROM CHARACTER ANALYSIS

Probably the greatest truth which I uncovered in my personal analysis work was the fact that most of those analyzed had not discovered the principle underlying the practice of rendering more service and better service than actually paid for.

The president of a correspondence school engaged me to analyze his employees. He was so impressed with the information disclosed in connection with this common weakness of giving as little as possible and demanding as much as possible, that he called me into his office and informed me that his employees were not the only ones in his organization who were guilty of this weakness; that the school, itself, had been guilty of the same mistake, and as a result of the fact disclosed, he intended to revise his educational system, not only giving his students more service and better service than they were paying for, but going still further and passing this same thought on to the students, through a specially designed lesson for that purpose, so that they, in turn, would render that sort of service.

Of the 10,000 people whom I have analyzed, I have never yet known of a single person who succeeded by delivering less service and of a poorer quality than that contracted for.

A young man whom I once analyzed was then working as a stenographer in the offices of the Pennsylvania Railroad Company. He had a very fine analysis with one exception. He said, "No, I do not believe in delivering more service or better service than is paid for, because my experience with the railroad company has taught me that this does not pay. They will keep a person in one job until they are gray-headed if they do their work well."

I had never seen this young man, but the photographs which he sent with his personal analysis chart disclosed the fact that he was a fine specimen, with broad, well-extended forehead, and an unusually large square jaw and chin, the positive, aggressive, fighting type.

Instead of reporting on his analysis by letter, as it was my custom to do in out of town cases, I wrote the young man and requested him to come to Chicago for a visit with me in person. He arrived one Sunday morning, and I met him at my house.

I told him a little story, after he was comfortably seated in the library, as follows:

"I have brought you all the way from Pittsburgh to tell you this little story, with the hope that it will be worth more to you than anything that ever happened in your life."

His face brightened up, and his eyes sparkled with anticipation as I proceeded.

"I once knew a young lad who worked in a coal mine. His job was that of water boy. After making his rounds with his water bucket, he would go over to the tipple and help the drivers out by hitching the mules to the empty cars that were to be hauled back into the mines, while the drivers were dumping the loaded cars.

"One day, the president of the company that owned the mines came along, saw this young lad, and asked him who gave him a driver's job. The lad replied, 'Nobody gave it to me. I just took it to keep me busy while I'm not carrying water.'

"He asked the lad how much he was getting for that extra work, to which he replied, 'Nothing! I like it!'

"Now, it may interest you to know that the president of that coal company took this lad out of the mines, gave him a job in the office, and arranged for him to attend night school. Today, he is known in every English-speaking country in the world and is recognized as one of the leading people in his line of work, all because he was willing to do more than he was paid for."

The young man's eyes dropped to the floor. He thought for several seconds, then looked up with a smile on his face, and said, "I understand the application! I will go back to Pittsburgh and make use of the point."

Today, this young man holds one of the most responsible jobs with one of the big packing houses of the country. Having made up his mind that the railroad business offered limited opportunity to put into practice the habit of performing more work and better work than is paid for, he changed jobs and went with a concern where he thought such service would be more quickly recognized. His rise was quick. He attributes his success entirely to that one single turning point in his life.

Character analysis is the most interesting work in the world. It uncovers the highlights of human nature and clearly shows those qualities which tear down as well as those which build up.

After analyzing a few thousand people, I learned to classify people as to certain tendencies just from their personal appearance, the lines in their faces, etc., before examining their analysis charts.

Crime and punishment grow out of the same stem.
Every principle can be used for either good or evil.

As an example of the characteristics which indicate one's tendencies, let me cite this case:

I once analyzed a man to whom I pointed out his chief weakness before he had taken his seat in my office, and before he had spoken more than a dozen words. When he announced himself, he said in a low, apologetic voice, "Pardon me for intruding, but I would like to know if you can tell why I don't get ahead in my job."

I looked up at the man. He was standing with his cap in his hands and with a look on his face which clearly showed that he lacked aggressiveness and self-confidence. He had even apologized for being in my office. It did not require very deep analysis to see that all who wished could ride that fellow and take advantage of him on every occasion.

As he took his seat, I replied to his question by saying:

"Yes, I can tell you one reason that you don't get ahead, and that is because you allow people to impose on you."

Quickly he asked, "Has my wife been telling you about me?"

I told him I had never seen his wife and did not even know his name; that I answered his question from what I saw written in his face, from the question which had been asked, the tone in which he had asked it, and his general demeanor, all of which clearly indicated that he permitted people to take advantage of him at will.

He admitted that my "guess" was a good one!

But it was no guess. There are certain tendencies so clearly written in the human face, in the voice, and in the personal carriage of one's body that all who will, may analyze and read.

In character analysis, I govern my recommendations largely by the law of cause and effect. I know what the chief causes for failure are, and I have found out how these causes may be replaced by those more desirable ones which ensure success.

It is a comparatively simple process to analyze and ascertain which particular negative causes are standing in a person's way, and when this analysis is made, the negative causes replaced by positive ones, the inevitable result is a change also in the effect from failure to success.

/ ENTREPRENEUR TIP

Identify what's standing in your way. What's getting in the way of feeling "settled" with yourself and your success journey? It just might be imposter syndrome, the belief that you are somehow not worthy of your success or that you are fooling everyone. How do you get past it? Start by incorporating some affirmative habits into your daily routine. Do some positive self-talk in the mirror each morning. Or, you can list two to three things that you have accomplished each day (or month, or year) so you can see the results of your efforts. Give yourself room to fail, and recognize that you are where you're meant to be.

Another startling thing that I have discovered from character analysis is the fact that, in most cases, only a comparatively slight change is necessary to replace failure with success.

No two cases can be handled in exactly the same manner. Usually, however, some more or less spectacular method must be employed in arousing a person sufficiently to "bounce" them out of the negative habit which is standing between them and success.

It is seldom sufficient merely to tell a person what is wrong and how to correct it. Some telling parallel must be drawn, some case cited, some illustration used which will show a person their own weaknesses by showing them the same weakness in another. The reason for this is simple; it is because most of us refuse to face facts concerning ourselves unless those facts are agreeable ones.

I have made several permanent and a considerably large number of temporary enemies by analyzing people and frankly telling them what the analysis disclosed, which, I am reminded to state, gave me another slant on human nature, namely that most of us love to be flattered, but seldom will we hear the truth without resentment if it happens not to appeal to our vanity.

May it not be possible that more cooperation and less competition among the masses would go a long way to emancipate the "salary bound?"

Once a man came to see me who wanted to change his trade to please his wife. He was a carpenter and had been working at that trade for ten years. He had done fairly well, having saved enough to build his own home. But his wife thought that carpentry was not the work for him, so she had urged him to take up "something more dignified."

His analysis clearly showed that he was engaged in the work most suitable for him, with the exception, possibly, that he could have advanced into contracting and building, thereby earning more money but still availing himself of his years of practical experience, without changing his line entirely.

In my analysis, I talked rather plainly about women who, for the sake of pride, try to urge a man to quit the work that has given him a living and jump, without preparation, into something in which he lacks experience, and for which he has no desire. My frankness made him angry. He went away, and I did not hear from him for several weeks. One afternoon, his wife came to see me. She said that he came home and told her, word-for-word, what I had said. At first, she was angered, but as she cooled down and thought it over, she saw the reason for my recommendation, and she, too, urged her husband to remain in his trade, but to take on a small contract and see what happened.

He had just completed his first contract, and the result was what brought her to my office. He had cleared a little over $1,100 on the job and was now engaged in business with a well-known contractor and builder who had a going business. They were both happy, and everything was lovely.

Some have gone away without coming back. Perhaps my frankness served them, maybe not. At any rate, I believe that the truth, even though it may hurt, is what a person ought to have when considering change in work or taking up a life work.

A person's work takes up six days out of every seven. If that work brings happiness and success, all well and good; but if not, then six-sevenths of that person's life is wasted.

I hope to see the time come when every public school will carefully chart and analyze every student who goes through, recommending at the end of the course the work which the student ought to give preference. I believe the time will arrive when this sort of service will be so strongly demanded that it will be supplied.

It would be impossible to be 100 percent perfect in these analyses on account of the youthfulness of the children, but they would form the foundation upon which a more accurate analysis could be made later on, after the child had worked long enough to bring out their natural tendencies, native ability, natural inclination, etc.

Under the simple system which I have employed in my character analysis work and personal analysis tests, I would guarantee a reasonable degree of success in every case analyzed if my recommendation were followed, providing the person analyzed is matured in age and has had opportunity to try his or her hand at a sufficient number of kinds of work to bring out natural tendencies and native ability.

❙ ENTREPRENEUR ACTION ITEM
Get Involved with Employee Development

In this essay, Hill models an approach that relies on strong emotional intelligence: knowing how to help others identify their strength so they succeed. That's a note all leaders and managers can take. After all, your job as a leader is making sure your team achieves their professional goals. Your team's success depends on your ability to help individual team members achieve their own successes. Talk with your highest performers about their long-term career goals, and identify ways that you can help these individuals move closer to them. Pinpoint the skills they need to make progress, and work together to find educational opportunities—whether that means conferences, seminars, classes, or additional responsibilities at work—that they can take advantage of in the months ahead.

Perhaps not everyone on your team is eager to chase professional growth. Some of your colleagues aren't sure what they need to do in order to advance their careers; others may not know where they want to be in the next two to five years. However, there's a good chance that your team members will respond positively if you challenge them to set professional development goals and show that you're interested in helping them meet them.

Personal Growth Means Company Growth

Many leaders fear that by investing in the development of their current employees, they're equipping them to snag better jobs elsewhere. But talented individuals want to be challenged; they expect employers to help them learn new skills and develop new capabilities. If you're not able or willing to do that, they'll find someone who is.

Simply put, companies that don't invest in their people aren't companies that smart people want to work for. Moreover, if your people aren't growing, it's very likely that your company isn't growing, either. In that case, competitors will indeed either overtake you or poach your top talent. Avoid both situations by taking the following steps heading into the new year.

1. Create a personal development plan for each employee.

Most of the factors that employees view as integral to engagement are related to professional and career development, according to the Society for Human Resource Management. Yet the employee satisfaction associated with these factors tends to be low. No two employees have the same professional vision, and many on your team will learn differently from others. With that in mind, offer a menu of development options, such as webinars, e-learning projects, books, and lectures.

2. Enrich employees' understanding of other departments.

Exposing your team members to the work that other teams or departments are doing is a great way to expand their understanding of their own work. Likewise, it allows you to introduce them to new challenges and possibly even help them discover new passions. Start by adding department presentations or one-on-one meetings to your new-hire onboarding. Also, highlight projects from various teams throughout the company in a monthly internal newsletter or in a weekly email focused on companywide wins.

There are plenty of reasons to cross-train employees. When team members can do each other's jobs, your company won't be in a bind if someone is out of the office or leaves abruptly. Just bear in mind that doing so requires a detailed plan.

3. Encourage employees to push each other forward.

Our personal growth often depends on the people surrounding us. After all, when workers want to learn a new skill, 55 percent will turn to their peers first, according to a Degreed study. And when we're among people who share a common objective, we tend to be more motivated than when we're chasing goals alone.

Implement pods of teams focused on similar goals or hold mastermind groups, which offer a forum for employees to share personal and business successes, as well as their goals. By assigning employees to small mastermind groups, you give them a peer group that's focused on holding them accountable to the development goals they've set.

No one's able to advance a career alone. Show the members of your team that you're willing to help them meet their professional goals. Your company's productivity and performance will reap the benefits.

CHAPTER ELEVEN

Success

Most of us are asking for success without the usual hardships which come with it. We want success with as little effort as possible.

May it not be well to define success, as we understand it, and write out a description of it as one of the items on our list of hoped-for achievements for the coming year? [Here, Hill is referring to the editors of his magazine.]

We do not know what your definition of the term success is, but if we may impose our own definition on you, we would do so as follows:

Success is the sum total of one's acts and thoughts which have, on account of their positive, constructive nature, brought happiness and good cheer to the majority of those with whom one has been associated in the past and the majority of those with whom one will be thrown in contact the coming year.

You cannot possibly bring happiness, good cheer, and sunshine into the lives of those with whom you associate and not enjoy success. Neither can you bring misery, despondency, and unhappiness to others and be a success.

If you cause other people to smile when you are near; if you carry with you that rich, vibrating, dynamic personality which causes people to be glad when you are near; if you speak and think of the beauties of life and persuade others to do the same; if you have eliminated cynicism, hatred, fear, and despondency from your own nature and filled their place with a wholesome love for all humanity, then you are bound to be a success.

l ENTREPRENEUR TIP

Incorporate joy into your business. There are many ways to create a real, authentic workspace for yourself and your colleagues and employees that go beyond birthday cake in the break room. Provide positive feedback regularly, have an open-door policy, engage with employees about topics that are important to them, and celebrate every win.

Money is not evidence of success! It may be, in fact, evidence of failure, and will be if happiness and goodwill do not accompany it throughout the process through which it was accumulated.

I value more highly than all the wealth in the world the pleasure—the thrilling joy—the happiness and contentment which has come to me as a result of the opportunity which I have had during the past year to serve my fellowmen through the pages of this magazine.

Could any amount of money buy such pleasure?

No! A thousand times, no! Pleasure comes from doing and not from acquiring. This is a lesson which some people seem never to learn, but it is a truth, nevertheless.

The roadway to that thing which we call success leads only in one direction, and that is straight through the great field of human service. Any road which leads in other directions cannot possibly reach success.

> ### ↗ ENTREPRENEUR TIP
> Be a servant leader. Believing in yourself or your business is a great feeling. So, why not share the wealth? Make a practice of sharing the power of belief with your employees, clients, and colleagues. Showing others you believe in them goes a long way toward fostering morale and a healthy company culture.

This writer intends to try to be happier this year than he was last, not by "acquiring" more worldly good, although he could use these to advantage, but by serving more people through this magazine and by bringing greater happiness to the members of his immediate family and his personal friends. If we cannot increase our measure of success in this manner, then we know not how to do so!

By no means do we recommend that anyone give up the pursuit of money as one means of finding success and happiness, but we strongly recommend that no one depend entirely upon the power of money for success.

We have never had enough money to cause us to quit trying to render service, but some whom we know have had, and the result was not what we call success.

FINANCIAL SUCCESS IS DANGEROUS

Financial success brings power, and power is a dangerous thing to those who have not learned how to use it justly and wisely. Great financial power has a decided tendency to develop intolerance and disregard for the rights of others. When you begin to succeed financially, you will need to watch your step more closely than ever before.

Financial success too often smothers the finer impulses of the human heart. It is the exception and not the rule when a person who accumulates great financial power without having tasted liberally of the dregs of poverty uses that power wisely.

Real success cannot be measured in dollars. It is something which can be measured only by the quantity and the quality of service which one renders for the good of others.

If financial power takes away the desire to render useful service, then it may be properly interpreted as failure instead of success.

We do not know for sure, but we strongly suspect that the only real success is that which brings happiness to oneself and to others. We also suspect that the only sure means of attaining happiness is through some sort of useful service which helps others to find happiness. Financial power doesn't always do this.

Watch your step as you begin to accumulate more money than you need for your daily use. Take care that it does not blind your eyes to the one sure pathway to real success, which is the performance of useful service for the good humanity.

THE GOLDEN RULE AS A BUSINESS WEAPON

It seems ridiculous to refer to the Golden Rule as a "weapon," but that is just what it is—a weapon which no resistance on earth can withstand.

The Golden Rule is a powerful weapon in business because there is so little competition in its application.

At the time of this writing, the whole world seems to have gone into the business of "profiteering," which means the same as "getting without giving fair value in return."

This spirit of greed cannot long prevail. What an opportunity, then, for the far-sighted people who will adopt the Golden Rule as their business motto now. The contrast would be so noticeable that it would excite widespread comment and bring all the business that could be handled; and long after the profiteers have gone out of business, those who have applied the Golden Rule would find that they had "built their houses upon a rock."

What a glorious opportunity the labor unions have to ride to victory— permanent, profitable, bloodless victory—by applying the Golden Rule and making it their motto. Will union labor be big enough to see this opportunity and utilize it? What an opportunity the present situation offers some person in the rank and file of labor to rise to leadership, not only of organized labor merely, but to the highest and most responsible leadership the American people have to offer, by influencing labor to conduct its affairs under the Golden Rule philosophy.

There is not a situation on earth which does not offer a splendid opportunity for someone to benefit by making use of the Golden Rule.

The time is not far distant when it will be business suicide to try to conduct business under any other standard except the Golden Rule. This fact is so obvious that it seems to this writer expedient for the wise ones to fall in line now and thereby get credit for something which they will later have to do anyway.

Adopt the Golden Rule as your business motto and write it on your business stationery and in every advertisement you publish. It will pay you handsomely.

MORE MERCY AND LESS JUSTICE

Throughout the universe, there is a tendency to "strike back." An eye for an eye and a tooth for a tooth is the practice.

Maybe it is necessary to mete out "justice" to people who make mistakes; maybe it is right for the "law" to exact its pound of flesh; but, mark this down as a sure thing—the law of retaliation is always and everywhere at work.

People "retaliate" in kind, just as surely as the sun rises in the east and sets in the west. It makes no difference that the law deals out "justice," those to whom it is dealt will "retaliate" in kind just as surely as there is a Master at the head of this universe.

If that is true, then may it not be well to temper justice with mercy? May it not be well to make the punishment fit the erring one instead of the crime?

Faith in the psychic? I am a thorough psychologist, believing that we are helped by influence beyond ourselves—Marie Corelli

Will "the people" continue to hound the unfortunate person who has made a mistake, thereby firmly fixing in their heart a determination to strike back, or will they someday learn that mercy and kindness awakes in the human heart the desire to retaliate in kind?

It is not justice that we need to dwell upon in our courts of criminal practice; it is mercy. Deal out justice, not to the erring person, but to the confirmed criminal. When you exact your pound of flesh from a person who has merely made a mistake, you run the risk of causing them to "strike back" so hard that they may become a criminal.

ENTHUSIASM

Enthusiasm is one of the most desirable of qualities. It attracts people to you and causes them to cooperate with you.

Enthusiasm is the spark which touches off that dormant power which is housed in your brain and puts it into action.

Enthusiasm is a sure antidote for laziness and procrastination; it is the main spring which keeps your mental machinery in action.

Enthusiasm overcomes despondency and generates hope, self-confidence, and courage. Enthusiasm stirs up your liver and puts it to work, thereby helping it carry on its vital function of cleansing your blood.

Enthusiasm arouses your whole being and causes you to transform your dreams into reality.

> *Somewhere in space, there exists the abiding place of ideas, and as fast as earth-dwellers are ready for them, they are released. Like a bird, the idea takes flight and seeks a home in the brain of someone who is singled out to forward it for the benefit of humanity.—Jennie June Croly*

If you are not enthusiastic over your work, you do not love it; therefore, you are trying to perform work for which you are not fitted.

Enthusiasm is contagious! Unconsciously, you pass it on to those with whom you come in contact, and it arouses them to act and think as you do.

An enthusiastic person, when guided by a sense of justice toward others, is usually a great asset in any organization, business, family, or community.

Are you a person of enthusiasm?

TWO ONE-LEGGED MEN

In the town of Wichita Falls, Texas, I saw a one-legged man sitting on the sidewalk begging for alms.

A few questions brought out the fact that he had a fair education. He said he was begging because no one would give him work. "The world is against me, and I have lost confidence in myself," he said.

Ah, there was the rub!

"I have lost confidence in myself."

Across the hall from my office is another one-legged man. I have known him for several years, and I know that his schooling was slight. He has less training than the one-legged beggar.

But, he is earning $1,000 a month. As sales manager of a manufacturing business, he is directing the efforts of 50 men.

The beggar displayed the stump of his amputated leg as evidence that he needs alms. The other one-legged man covered up the stump of his lost leg so it would not attract attention.

The difference between the two men exists merely in viewpoint. One believes in himself, and the other does not! The one who believes in himself could give up the other leg and both of his arms and still earn a thousand dollars a month. He could even give up both eyes, to boot, and still earn the money.

The world never defeats you until you defeat yourself. Milo C. Jones of "Little Pig Sausage" fame became a wealthy person out of the sausage business after paralysis had taken away the use of nearly every muscle in his body. He couldn't turn over in bed without aid.

As long as you have faith in yourself and that wonderful mind of yours continues to function properly, you cannot be defeated in any legitimate undertaking. This statement is made without qualifications because it is true.

/ ENTREPRENEUR ACTION ITEM
Model Success for Your Team

Success isn't magic, as Hill points out here. It's all about the execution of good habits and building an atmosphere of success for yourself and those who work with and for you. As a leader, whether you're leading a small group or a large corporation, you can help set your team up for success.

The struggles of first-time leaders are both real and widespread. New leaders are thrown into the deep end to sink or swim. They either figure out how to become a successful leader or fail and retreat disillusioned back to individual contributors and unlikely to step up to a leadership role again.

How often do you see high-performing individuals promoted into leadership roles? The skills that enabled an individual to perform at a high level are rarely the same ones that will support them as an influential leader. When people choose to step into a leadership role, they are more likely to bring the right attitude and behaviors that breed success.

Stepping into a leadership role is one of the most courageous decisions in one's career. In today's digital world, a new kind of leader is required. A leader who consistently leads others by supporting people and the organization to grow intentionally through pursuing goals that stretch their skills, collaborating and fostering interdependence, opening doors of opportunity for others, and a commitment and passion for becoming better leaders.

No one is immune to facing new challenges. New leaders must understand the problems, identify what needs to be done now, and how they can impact the organization. Here are 12 ways first-time leaders can take themselves to the next level.

1. Never Underestimate the Transition

Many organizations do not provide the support required to enable leaders to transition into a first-time leadership position successfully. Globoforce reported that 47 percent of managers don't receive any training when they take a new leadership role. Development and eLearning programs must be in place months before the transition to build leadership skills while being coached regularly.

2. Have Great Conversations

Interacting effectively with others creates environments where both leaders and teams are engaged and inspired. The quality of interactions affects how people feel about themselves, their leader, and being part of the team.

Harvard Business Review published recent research supporting that leaders who listen well are perceived as people leaders, generate more trust, instill higher job satisfaction, and increase their team's creativity. Leaders stepping into these roles must ask themselves, "Am I a good listener?" Because if you are going to lead, you must be.

A study published in the *Personality and Social Psychology Bulletin* showed that organizations either have a growth or fixed mindset. Carol

Dweck, who was part of the research team, confirmed that whichever the leader chooses to practice will flow to the employees, how they see the company and act within.

3. Leadership is a Never-Ending Journey

Organizations can support the development of leadership skills by focusing on building leadership development journeys that span multiple years. Like all professionals, leadership requires continued opportunities for practice, skill-building, and real-world experiences. The organization must provide the tools and culture to make this happen. By proactively seeking out experiences to apply skills and building a habit of collecting feedback on progress, they position themselves as a self-driven leader and embody self-reflection on how they can improve.

4. There is No Endpoint

No leader ever reaches the finishing point. Even when leaders become an authority or thought leader in their industry, the environment in which they operate would more than likely continue to change. Leaders must create a new set of expectations and develop new skills to continue to have a presence and impact. AT&T continuously train their employees to ensure they have the skills the company needs to succeed in an ever-changing world.

5. Leaders Work for Their People

Most first-time managers think that stepping into a leadership role is graduation. The truth is it is the starting point. As a leader, you must understand what your employees want at a deep level and can adapt to their needs. Different needs drive each person. For some, people are driven by status and money; others by wanting to spend more time with their family or others may wish to broaden experience and work in a global office.

By delving into what intrinsically motivates your people, first-time leaders increase their emotional intelligence by listening, empathizing, and empowering their people. The best leaders are the most excellent mentors as they take all the blame and give all the credit away.

6. Impact with Kindness

When it comes to leading a team, compassion and empathy are underrated qualities. If first-time leaders are secure within themselves, they will build other people up instead of tearing them down.

When you care about your people at a deep level, you sit in the winner's seat. Companies that have all the tools and software in the world to monitor how people are traveling, yet if they genuinely do not care about their people, they will ultimately fail.

People demand authenticity and transparency within the workplace. Positivity, kindness, and empathy must be the foundation of how you deliver conversations. Instilling characteristics as part of your culture has a long-term impact on your business.

7. Trust is Your Most Valuable Asset

How often do you hear the manager placing restrictions around their employees and then left them once they have "earned" the trust of the leader? Many managers are either afraid of short-term losses that come with giving trust or fearful that their employees will be better than them, so fear becomes the common denominator informing their decisions. What if we flipped this belief and embraced unlimited trust as the foundation of any professional relationship at the beginning and then slowly take that trust away if they do something to lose it.

8. Have Courageous Conversations

When dealing with underperforming people who have talent, then managers must look at the infrastructure that supports their people to shine. Maybe the person sits in the wrong department; perhaps the manager hasn't asked the right questions. What is more important is how you have a conversation with the employee about how the leader and company can help them succeed. The onus sits with the leader. Leaders create rules and have the power to change them.

9. Improve the Employee Experience

It is the leader's responsibility to reframe focus on longer-term objectives. Leaders must encourage employees to do more of what they do best while facilitating on how they can improve areas of development. Making your comments specific and actionable, allows the employee to hear constructive feedback that can lead to positive change. The more you listen to your people before giving feedback, the better the employee experience.

When you deliver feedback, focus on discussing what happened, stick to the facts instead of focusing on how the employee did something wrong. It is a perfect opportunity for a leader to co-create solutions with the employee in their journey of change.

10. Schedule One-on-One Time

Gallup revealed that employees whose managers hold regular meetings are almost three times as likely to be engaged as employees whose managers don't. Hosting weekly one-on-one meetings strengthens relationships between the leader and their team members, builds team loyalty, and they take the guesswork out of leadership. When you invest time to get to know your people well, unfiltered conversations provide great conversations for you to make informed, forward-thinking decisions as a leader to drive exceptional results.

11. Listening Conveys Trust

Influential leaders embrace responsibility for their whole team to succeed in their roles. While many assume being a boss means having all the answers, courageous leaders engage employees to share their ideas and solutions before jumping in. When leaders invest time and energy into discussing new goals and how to develop new skills, the leader marries company objectives with individual goals to ensure all benefits.

12. Leaders Create Leaders

The ultimate gift a leader can give is to create another first-time leader that replaces you. Paying this forward creates an opportunity for individual contributors to stand up and be seen. Leaders create more leaders, and providing the opportunity for another human being to embrace a level of fulfillment that comes from leadership is an incredible gift.

CHAPTER TWELVE

Your Personal Success Profile Questionnaire

The following principles of personal achievement have been responsible for the success of the world's outstanding leaders. Success is a science and you can learn its secrets regardless of your personal occupation, environment, or residence. You must answer these 75 questions honestly if you wish to succeed. The answers to these questions reveal you, the true you, as an individual who is utterly different from any other person on earth. The answers form a searching analysis of you and your ambitions. The answers give you facts about yourself that will amaze you.

Simply answer each question honestly, then score your answers and total your score to discover your rating.

THE 17 PRINCIPLES OF PERSONAL ACHIEVEMENT

These 17 principles have been responsible for the success of the world's outstanding leaders. Success is a science, and you can learn its secrets regardless of your present occupation, environment, and residence. You may be a highly regarded successful businessperson now, or you may be a poorly paid factory worker. You may live in a big city, or you may live on a farm miles from the nearest town; it makes no difference. You can learn the secrets of success, and your honest answers to these questions are the first step for you to take.

Definiteness of Purpose

Have you decided upon a definite goal in life? ☐ YES ☐ NO
Have you set a date for reaching that goal? ☐ YES ☐ NO
Do you have a specific plan for achieving your goal in life? ☐ YES ☐ NO
Have you determined what definite benefits your goal in life will bring
you? ☐ YES ☐ NO

Mastermind Alliance

Are other people helping you to attain your goal in life? ☐ YES ☐ NO
Do you believe that a person can succeed in life without the aid of others?
☐ YES ☐ NO
Do you believe you can readily succeed in your occupation if you
are opposed by your spouse or other members of your family?
☐ YES ☐ NO
Are there certain advantages when an employer and an employee work
together in harmony? ☐ YES ☐ NO

Applied Faith

Do you have faith in Infinite Intelligence? ☐ YES ☐ NO
Do you have confidence in your ability to do anything you desire?
☐ YES ☐ NO
Are you entirely free from all of these seven basic fears? ☐ YES ☐ NO
Do you have a fear of poverty, criticism, ill health, loss of love, loss of
liberty, old age, death? ☐ YES ☐ NO

Going the Extra Mile

Do you make a habit of rendering more service than you are paid to do?
☐ YES ☐ NO

Do you believe there are times when an employee is entitled to ask for
more pay? ☐ YES ☐ NO

Do you know of anyone who has achieved success in any calling without
doing more than they were paid to do? ☐ YES ☐ NO

Do you believe anyone has a right to ask for an increase in salary unless
they are doing more than they are paid for? ☐ YES ☐ NO

If you were an employer, would you be satisfied with the sort of service you
are now rendering as an employee? ☐ YES ☐ NO

Attractive Personality

Do you have habits which offend others? ☐ YES ☐ NO

Are you liked by those with whom you work? ☐ YES ☐ NO

Can you interest people when speaking in public? ☐ YES ☐ NO

Are there times when you seem to bore others? ☐ YES ☐ NO

Personal Initiative

Do you plan your own work each day? ☐ YES ☐ NO

Do you have to have your work planned for you? ☐ YES ☐ NO

Do you have certain outstanding qualities which are not possessed by
others in your line of work? ☐ YES ☐ NO

When your plans fail, do you give up? ☐ YES ☐ NO

Do you ever create better plans for doing your work more efficiently?
☐ YES ☐ NO

Positive Mental Attitude

Do you know what is meant by a positive mental attitude? ☐ YES ☐ NO

Can you control your mental attitude at will? ☐ YES ☐ NO

Do you know what you have complete control over? ☐ YES ☐ NO

Do you know how to detect a negative mental attitude in others?
☐ YES ☐ NO

Do you have a method of developing the habit of positive mental attitude?
☐ YES ☐ NO

Enthusiasm

Are you known as a person of enthusiasm? ☐ YES ☐ NO

Can you control your enthusiasm by applying it in carrying out your plans?
☐ YES ☐ NO

Does your enthusiasm sometimes become the master of your judgment?
☐ YES ☐ NO

Self-Discipline

Do you hold your tongue when angry? ☐ YES ☐ NO

In a heated discussion, do you speak before you think? ☐ YES ☐ NO

Do you lose your patience easily? ☐ YES ☐ NO

Are you even-tempered at all times? ☐ YES ☐ NO

Do you allow your affections to sway your judgment? ☐ YES ☐ NO

Accurate Thinking

Do you make it your duty to learn what others know in connection with
your occupation, which may be of value to you? ☐ YES ☐ NO

Do you express opinions on subjects with which you are not familiar?
☐ YES ☐ NO

Do you know how to acquire facts in connection with any subject in which
you are interested? ☐ YES ☐ NO

Controlled Attention

Do you concentrate all your thoughts on whatever you are doing?
☐ YES ☐ NO

Are you easily influenced to change your plans or your decision?
☐ YES ☐ NO

Are you inclined to abandon your aims and plans when you meet
opposition? ☐ YES ☐ NO

Do you become interested in other people and their plans as quickly as you
do in connection with yourself and your own ideas? ☐ YES ☐ NO

Teamwork

Do you get along harmoniously with others under all circumstances?
☐ YES ☐ NO

Do you grant favors as freely as you ask for them? ☐ YES ☐ NO

Do you have continual disagreements with others on certain subjects? ☐ YES ☐ NO

Do you believe there are advantages in friendly cooperation with those with whom you work? ☐ YES ☐ NO

Are you aware of the damage you can cause yourself and your fellow employees by not cooperating with coworkers? ☐ YES ☐ NO

Learning from Adversity and Defeat

Does defeat cause you to stop trying? ☐ YES ☐ NO

If you fail in a given effort, do you begin again with a new plan? ☐ YES ☐ NO

Do you believe that temporary defeat can become failure? ☐ YES ☐ NO

Have you learned any lessons from defeat? ☐ YES ☐ NO

Do you know how defeat can be converted into an asset that may lead to success? ☐ YES ☐ NO

Creative Vision

Is your imagination keen and alert? ☐ YES ☐ NO

Do you make your own decisions? ☐ YES ☐ NO

Do you prefer to call on others for their opinions before you act? ☐ YES ☐ NO

Have you ever invented anything? ☐ YES ☐ NO

Do you create practical ideas readily in connection with your work? ☐ YES ☐ NO

Do you believe that a person who creates ideas quickly is worth more than a person who follows only the ideas and plans created by others? ☐ YES ☐ NO

Maintain Sound Health

Do you know the essential factors of sound health? ☐ YES ☐ NO

Do you know what sound health begins with? ☐ YES ☐ NO

Do you know what relation relaxation has to sound health? ☐ YES ☐ NO

Do you know how to balance sound health? ☐ YES ☐ NO

Can you explain hypochondria? ☐ YES ☐ NO

Budgeting Time and Money

Do you save a definite amount of your income? ☐ YES ☐ NO

Do you spend money without considering what would happen if your income were cut off? ☐ YES ☐ NO

Do you get sufficient sleep each night? ☐ YES ☐ NO

Do you spend all your spare time having fun? ☐ YES ☐ NO

Habits

Do you have habits which you feel you cannot control? ☐ YES ☐ NO

Have you had undesirable habits which you have eliminated? ☐ YES ☐ NO

In the past few months, have you developed any new, desirable habits?
☐ YES ☐ NO

Here's how to rate your answers

All of the following questions should have been answered "NO":
2b, 2c, 4c, 4d, 5a, 5d, 6b, 6d, 8c, 9b, 9c, 9e, 10b, 11b, 11c, 12c, 13a, 13c, 14c, 16b, 16d, 17a

All other questions should have been answered "YES."

Your score would have been 75 if all of the questions have been answered "NO" or "YES" as shown above. This is a perfect score, and very few people have ever made such a score. Now let's see what your score actually is.

"Yes" answers instead of "No" _____# of Wrong Answers

"No" answers instead of "Yes" _____# of Wrong Answers

Add the two totals together and subtract 75. This will be your score. Find your rating below:

75 points: Perfect (very rare)

66 to 75 points: Good (above average)

51 to 65 points: Fair (average)

26 to 50 points: Poor (below average)

25 points and below: Unsatisfactory

What Was Your Score?

If your score was average or even below average remember that most people answering this questionnaire had similar scores. The reason, of course, is that few individuals have been trained to grasp the secrets of success, the secrets that have lifted thousands upon thousands of average people to business and social leadership. There are no mental, physical, educational, or age barriers to these secrets of success. Success is a science, and its secrets are available to you if you want them.

YOU HAVE THE KEY TO SUCCESS WITHIN YOURSELF

Every person has hidden abilities within themselves. Most people are not even aware of them. Many people who have made outstanding successes of their lives discover these abilities by accident. Sometimes years of their lives have been wasted simply because they did not know they had great abilities. Accidents revealed these hidden abilities to them, and nothing on earth could hold them back after that. Success and happiness were theirs forevermore.

You can profit by their experience. No person should depend upon accident or fate to guide their success and happiness. Furthermore, accident or fate to guide success is reckless and careless; they do not always reveal to people the powerful hidden abilities they possess. Every person possesses them. They need only to be brought to the light of day, and acted upon. This you can do, just as thousands upon thousands of other people have done by studying the Napoleon Hill principles.

These principles are for you. They worked originally for the Greats . . . today, thousands of people are applying these same principles to achieve happiness, health, and wealth. People of all ages, people from all walks of life, are benefiting from these principles . . . SO CAN YOU!

❙ ENTREPRENEUR ACTION ITEM
Fuel Your Success with Self-Awareness

An African proverb says, "When there is no enemy within, the enemies outside can do you no harm."

Answering Hill's questionnaire is an exercise in self-awareness. If you took the time to reflect on your answers to these questions, perhaps some of your answers surprised you. When you practice the concept of self-awareness, you often find that you have areas you can work on to not only improve your daily life, but your mindset as well. Self-awareness is one of the most important skills for success. How you behave and respond to external situations is governed by internal mental processes. Self-awareness uncovers any destructive thought-patterns and unhealthy habits. This leads to better decision-making and behavioral responses.

Here are 12 exercises for greater self-awareness:

1. The Three Why's

Before acting on a decision, ask yourself "Why?" Follow up your response with another "Why?" And then a third. If you can find three good reasons to pursue something, you'll have clarity and be more confident in your actions.

Being self-aware means knowing your motives and determining whether they're reasonable.

2. Expand Your Emotional Vocabulary

The philosopher Wittgenstein said, "The limits of my language means the limits of my world."

Emotions create powerful physical and behavioral responses that are more complex than "happy" or "sad." Putting your feelings into words has a therapeutic effect on your brain; if you're unable to articulate how you feel, that can create stress. Determine your list of "feeling words" to help with labeling your emotions. Increase your emotional vocabulary with one new word each day.

3. Practice Saying No

The ability to say "no" to yourself to put off short-term gratification for the long-term gain is an important life skill. Like a muscle, it is strengthened with exercise. The more you practice saying "no" to small daily challenges, the better you can withstand major temptations.

There are plenty of daily temptations—social media, junk food, gossiping, YouTube. Make a goal of saying "no" to five different temptations each day.

4. Break Visceral Reactions

A person without self-awareness runs on auto-pilot, and responds with knee-jerk reactions. Self-awareness allows you to assess situations objectively and rationally, without acting on biases and stereotypes.

Take a deep breath before you act, especially when a situation triggers anger or frustration. This gives you time to re-assess whether your response will be the best one.

5. Be Accountable

Nobody is perfect. Being aware of your flaws, but failing to accept accountability is leaving the job half-done. We're often critical of others, while ignorant of our own flaws. Self-awareness helps turn the mirror on ourselves and prevents hypocritical behavior.

Iteration and self-improvement only happens once you recognize a flaw. Create a habit of acknowledging your mistakes, rather than making excuses.

6. Monitor Your Self-Talk

There is non-stop commentary in our heads that is not always helpful. A little bit of negative self-talk can spiral into stress and depression.

Pay attention to the way you respond to your successes and failures—do you pass off your achievements as luck? And crucify yourself after failures? Positive and negative feedback-loops will form in your mind based off how you respond to successes and failures. Being tough on yourself needs to be balanced with self-compassion. Celebrate your wins, forgive your losses.

7. Improve Body Language Awareness

Watching yourself on video can be a cringeworthy experience, but awareness of your body language, posture, and mannerisms improves your confidence.

Slouching, or taking a "low-power-pose" increases cortisol and feeds low self-esteem, while standing tall or taking a "high-power-pose" stimulates testosterone and improves your performance. Using hand gestures helps with articulating your thoughts and affects how people respond to you.

Record a speech or presentation and evaluate your posture and hand gestures. Watch videos of skilled speakers and adopt their mannerisms to improve your own.

8. Play "Devil's Advocate."

Taking an opposing view forces you to question your assumptions. Your "default" beliefs and worldview are not always reasonable; it's healthy to "argue against yourself" and see how your views hold up.

And you'll give your brain a good workout. Processing challenging information stimulates new neural connections.

9. Know Your Personality Type

Knowing your personality type allows you to maximize your strengths and manage your weaknesses. Understanding your "strengths" and "talents" can be the difference between a good choice, and a *great* choice. (Strengths are skills and knowledge that can be acquired, while talents are innate).

Start with understanding where you fall on the introvert/extrovert spectrum; know your Myers-Briggs type; and then conduct a personal SWOT analysis (strengths, weaknesses, opportunities, threats).

10. Practice Self-Evaluation and Reflection

Keep a journal and track your progress. How would you rate your current level of self-awareness out of ten? Think about how often you say regretful things; repeat bad habits; make absent-minded decisions; and have erratic thoughts.

Set regular goals, break big goals down into smaller milestones. Ask yourself at the end of each day, "What did I do well today?" And, "How can I improve on this tomorrow?"

11. Ask for Constructive Feedback

We all have blind spots in our thinking patterns and behaviors. Asking for regular constructive feedback cuts through any self-deceit or one-dimensional views you might hold. But only ask people you'd consider mentors — those who understand you, whom you respect, and will tell you what you need to hear, not what you *want* to hear.

12. Meditate

Meditation is a foundational practice for improving self-awareness. To focus solely on your breathing is to focus on a key internal process. You'll become aware of how your mind wanders, and get better at snapping out of distractions.

For beginners, start with 10-minute sessions. Find a quiet place to sit, breath in through your nose and out through your mouth. Count your breaths silently, pulling your mind back when it wanders. See how many breaths you can string together.

Contemplative Philosophical In-Depth Reflections by Napoleon Hill

EDITOR'S NOTE: *We close out this book of selections from Napoleon Hill's First Editions with a collection of some of his most evergreen reflections on life, habits, work, and success. These reflections may be familiar to you if you have read Hill's works, as they reverberate throughout his entire body of work. As you read, you will see that Hill often used storytelling and verse to convey the points he was trying to make, perhaps as a way to engage his reader in a different way that was somewhat less heavy-handed than a traditional essay.*

ACHIEVEMENT IS BORN OF SACRIFICE

There can be no great achievement without a corresponding sacrifice. Think of one person, if you can, who has risen to fame or rendered the world a lasting service without sacrifice. Usually the value of the service rendered is in proportion to the sacrifice out of which it sprung.

Nature does not appear to favor the perpetuation of ideas or ideals which are not born of sacrifice and nurtured amid hardship and struggle. From the lowest mineral substance to the highest form of animal organism, nature gives evidence aplenty of her favoritism for that which is born of hardship, resistance, and struggle.

The hardiest and finest trees of the forest are those which grew slowly and overcame the greatest resistance. No hot-house vegetable can equal those that are grown in the open, in opposition to the elements of the weather.

In a practical, material world of business, finance, and industry, we see evidence on every hand of the soundness of this philosophy. Successes that are achieved overnight seldom endure. The greatest achievements in business are those which began at the very bottom, were based upon sound fundamentals, and experienced seemingly impossible sacrifice. Before we envy Henry Ford his success, we should meditate upon the struggles and hardships which he survived before he created the first Ford automobile. All of us would enjoy his great wealth, but few of us would be willing to pay for it in sacrifice, as he has done.

If you are taking your baptism of fire and paying the price of sacrifice with faith in your handiwork, no matter what station in life you are striving to achieve, you are apt to realize it if you carry on without losing faith, without turning back, without losing confidence in yourself and in the fundamental principle which insures achievement that corresponds to the nature and extent of your sacrifice.

I ENTREPRENEUR TIP

Sacrifice doesn't mean you have to give everything up to achieve success. But, think about what is holding you back in your business. That's what you should sacrifice—the things you don't need or that inhibit your ability to grow.

THE APPLIED GOLDEN RULE

During these times of lack of harmony among people and nations, when the world is rocked with chaos and strife and lack of faith, what greater work could a person engage in than that of planting constructive thoughts where destructive ones grew before? You have influence with a certain number of people, and if you wish to exercise that influence so it will bring you the greatest return in happiness and in fortune, you will lay aside all hatred or prejudice which may have fastened itself upon you and devote every ounce of your influence to helping people see the folly of strife and struggle and destructive effort. In thus wielding your influence for good, you may be sure that your efforts will return to you, like a boomerang, not to curse but to bless you and yours, for as surely as the sun rises in the east and sets in the west, the world will hand you back that which you hand it. You can be a person with a grievance or a person with a message; you can be a BUILDER or a DESTROYER, but make sure of this, that you can no more tear down without in turn being torn down, than you could sow wild mustard and reap a harvest of oats.

Applying the Golden Rule

EDITORIAL NOTE FROM NAPOLEON HILL: *The following letter was written by the editor of this magazine to a person who, without knowing the facts of which they spoke or the person of whom they spoke, had indulged in slanderous remarks which might have been answered more severely.*

While I have never met you in person, I feel that I know you through a mutual friend who has heard you speak of me.

The other day, a person asked me what I believed to be the greatest work a person could engage in, and my reply was this:

In this strife-ridden, grief-stricken world as she stands today, when so many are devoting their efforts to trying to tear somebody or something down, and to setting person against man, nation against nation, race against race, and creed against creed, and rekindling the fires of hate and prejudice and ignorance of the dark ages, it seems to me, brother, that the greatest work any person could engage in is that of planting constructive thoughts where destructive ones grew before.

I am doing my very best in person and through my magazine to plant as many such thoughts as I can, as I tarry by the wayside of life, and no one can recall a word or act of mine, unless in self-defense or in defense of a principle, which did not have as its aim the bringing together of people in a spirit of friendly cooperation, in a sincere effort to ameliorate the hardships of humanity and make this old world a brighter spot on which to live during the brief sojourn called life.

Many of my experiences, however, make it necessary for me to turn often to those beautiful words of our greatest American, the immortal Lincoln, when he said, "I do the best I know, the very best I can, and I mean to keep right on doing so until the end. If the end brings me out all right, what is said against me won't amount to anything. If the end brings me out wrong, 10 angels swearing I was right would make no difference."

I hope that someday our paths may cross in person. I am sure we would find that each of us is gifted with some of both the good and the bad traits of mankind.

Cordially and fraternally yours,

Napoleon Hill

ART THOU THE MAN?

These are times which test strength of civilization. That we may more easily re-establish our confidences in mankind, let us turn back the pages of history and study the philosophy of those who led us through similar disturbances which tried people's faith in each other.

Let us turn, in these days of reconstruction, to the beloved Lincoln, the great commoner, and in our imagination, let us hear him as he admonishes us to place the interests of the human race above those of the individual.

As we think about the rugged face of this great person who led the American people through the most trying period of their existence, let us not forget those fundamental qualities which distinguished him.

Lincoln should be a constant reminder that neither lowly birth nor poverty can permanently withhold fame and fortune from the person who keeps faith with those to whom they pledge their word to serve.

Every bank clerk and every graduate and every laborer and every person who serves in any capacity whatsoever should turn, often, to the memory of Lincoln and study the simplicity of which his greatness was born.

This man of destiny, born in a humble log cabin, set an example that we could all emulate to the everlasting glory of humankind when he demonstrated his love for the unpretentious things of life.

In this great economic struggle that is going on in the world today between capital and labor, both sides might profit by the thought that Lincoln needed neither the power of capital nor the force of the unions to carry him to the highest place within the gift of the American people. Might it not be possible that both union labor and capital would find it profitable to study and emulate the immortal Lincoln?

What a blessing if, out of the dim shadows of the past, the spirit of this great American would rise and spread its beneficent wings over the disgruntled, unsettled humanity, and lead the world back to an understanding of those simple truths which made Lincoln our greatest American.

Perhaps we have someone in our midst who is capable of following the guiding hand of such a spirit. Could it possibly do any harm if each of us searched his own heart with the question, "Art thou the man?"

BRACE UP

Brace up and stop worrying. The game of life is never lost until you accept defeat. Trusted friends will fail you as they have failed others before your time. You will try and fail and try and fail again, as millions of others have done. Waste no time fretting about this. It is only a repetition of that which has been taking place all back down the ages. You can wear only one suit of clothes at a time, and you can eat only one plate of ham and eggs at a sitting. And the things you worry about probably will never happen, and, if they did, you would not know the difference a hundred years from now; therefore, sit down in some quiet spot and calm yourself while the thought soaks into your head that the best policy is to take life as it comes without permitting anything or anyone either to break your heart or overwhelm you with joy.

ENTREPRENEUR TIP

Worry only begets worry. As entrepreneurs, we have plenty of reasons to lose sleep. To get out of your worry rut, focus on what is present in your life now. Name five things you know are solid and repeat them to ground yourself.

THE DREAMERS

Civilization owes its existence to the dreamers of the past. Civilization cannot advance ahead of its idealists and dreamers.

They are the pattern makers of humankind. The seething masses have always followed the paths which the dreamers have hewn.

Now the dreamers are about to take the glory out of conquest and war. Woodrow Wilson sacrificed himself as a target when he made the first step in stripping conquerors of their glory. Soon other dreamers will dare to follow the trail he has opened, and war will then be a disgrace, and those who advocate or engage in it will be social outcasts and brigands.

Even the individual who cherishes a lofty ideal in their heart is apt to realize it. Cherish your visions and your dreams for they are the blueprints of your ultimate attainment.

Your dreams can carry you to any station in life you cherish. If you are unworthy of the position you seek, remember that your aspirations and your dreams, operating through the law of auto-suggestion, can rebuild your character and *make you worthy*.

The White House is none too high as a mark of attainment for which to strive. Include it in your dreams, and you have already taken the first step toward realization.

EVERY FAILURE AND EVERY MISTAKE

Has it ever occurred to you that every failure and every mistake from which you survive and every obstacle which you master develops in you wisdom, strategy, and self-mastery, without which you could accomplish no great undertaking?

No person likes to meet with failure, yet every failure can be turned into a stepping stone that would carry one to the heights of achievement, if the lessons taught by the failure are organized, classified, and used as a guide.

If your failures embitter you toward others and develop cynicism in your heart, they will soon destroy your usefulness; but if you accept them as necessary teachers and build them into a shield, you can make of them an impenetrable protection.

Vanity prompts us to give more thought to our triumphs than we do to our failures; yet, if we profit by the experience of those who have accomplished most in the world, we will see that a person never needs to watch themselves so closely as when they begin to attain success, because success often causes a slackening of effort and a letting down of that eternal vigilance which causes a person to throw the power of their combative nature into that which they are doing.

⫽ ENTREPRENEUR TIP

Many entrepreneurs know failure like an old friend. And that's OK. Failure is where we learn; it's where you can gather the lessons and apply them to your next business, task, or idea.

HOPE

Do the thing and you shall have the power.—Emerson

The way of success is the way of struggle.

Lincoln wrote the greatest speech ever delivered in the English language on the back of an envelope a few moments before it was delivered, yet the thought of that speech was borne of hardship and struggle.

All down the road of life, you will meet with obstacles, many of them. Failure will overtake you time after time, but remember that it is a part of nature's method to place obstacles and failure in your way, as hurdles are placed before a horse that is being trained, that you may learn from these some of the greatest of all lessons.

Every time you master failure, you become stronger and better prepared to meet the next one. The moments of trial will come to you as they come to all at one time or another. Doubt and lack of faith in yourself and in your fellowmen will cast their dark shadows over you, but remember that the manner in which you react under these trying negatives will indicate whether you are developing power or slipping backward.

"And this, too, will soon pass," some people say. Nothing is permanent; therefore, why permit disappointment, resentment, or a keen sense of injustice to undermine your composure, because they will soon eliminate themselves.

Look back over your past, and you will see that those experiences of yesterday which bore heavily on your heart at the time and seemed to end all hope of success, passed away, and left you wiser than you were before.

The whole universe is in a constant state of flux. You are in a constant state of change. Evolution is removing the wounds left in your heart by disappointment. You need not go down under any difficulty if you but bear in mind that, "This, too, will soon pass."

HOW TO THINK ACCURATELY

The difference between the person who succeeds and the person who fails is largely determined by the manner in which each thinks. Accurate thought is a matter of habit and can be developed by any normal person who has the strength of character to demand it of themselves.

The art of accurate thought is comparatively simple, yet but few have mastered it. Practically all noteworthy achievement is built upon a foundation of accurate thought.

There are two steps which one must take in the process of thinking accurately. First, one must learn to separate facts from mere information. No one can become an accurate thinker if they rely upon hearsay evidence or whisperings of the winds of gossip. No one who accepts that which they read in the daily press as fact can hope to become an accurate thinker, because the press is not always based upon facts.

After the facts in a given circumstance have been obtained, they must be divided into two classes, namely relevant and irrelevant, or important and unimportant. No one can be an accurate and efficient thinker until they have learned how to separate facts into these two classes.

After this distinction has been made, one must cast aside the unimportant, superfluous, detailed facts and devote their time to building a definite plan of action out of the important facts in connection with a given circumstance.

This, in the main, is the simple process of accurate thinking.

When you hear a person say, "I see in the news" that "X" is a criminal because someone has charged him with dishonesty and makes no attempt to get the facts, you may know without asking that they are not an accurate thinker.

That the world's most successful people have been those who reserved their opinions until they were sure they had facts upon which to base opinions is well worth remembering.

An accurate thinker has many advantages over the person who is swayed, like a dry leaf on the bosom of a stray wind, by hearsay evidence and idle gossip. Among other advantages, they enjoy that of self-confidence because of their knowledge that they have searched until they got the facts. A person who goes after the facts and stays on the job until they get them is a hard person to defeat; on the other hand, the person who forms judgment out of mere information practically defeats themselves to start with.

On the walls of the office of a well-known person who has made several millions out of the steel business hangs a single card with this line in bold letters: GET THE FACTS!

Not a bad sign for the remainder of us to keep before us. Think about it the next time you find yourself acting without being sure of your facts.

If I were permitted to suggest a slight change in this card, I would word it this way:

GET THE FACTS AND ASSORT THEM.

This would naturally suggest the elimination of the lesser-important facts. It would lead, eventually, to the habit of accurate thinking.

Go back into your memory and you will find, more than likely, that most of your mistakes could have been avoided had you followed this practice of getting the facts. If one neighbor slanders another, get the facts. If someone offers you what they recommend as a fine investment, get the facts. This habit of getting the facts will save you many a grief. It will develop you, finally, into an accurate thinker.

/ ENTREPRENEUR TIP

Critical thinking is an important life skill. Seek out reliable sources of news and information from well-vetted outlets before you form an opinion.

THE LAW OF COMPENSATION

Take what figure you will, its exact value, no more nor less, still returns to you.—Emerson

Time brings us mighty evidences of the existence of the Law of Compensation [Most famously written about by Ralph Waldo Emerson, the Law of Compensation says that we get out of the universe what we put into it.]. Justice is never defeated; it is often postponed.

A true perspective of the Law of Compensation can only be gained by considering time and space. Rewards for virtue and punishment for wrongdoing are often withheld for years and even from one generation to another.

Generally, however, the Law of Compensation works with comparative swiftness. By and large, we reap that which we sow. A person may be a cheat and a fraud and seem to be getting away with the fruits of their stealthy practices, but there comes a time when they pay dearly through the loss of confidence and the withholding of friendliness by their neighbors.

On the other hand, a person may practice the Golden Rule for a long period of time and still seem to fail to reap the fruits of their ethical conduct, but who can say how much they will be paid in happiness which they would not have enjoyed but for this practice. It is the exception and not the rule when the world neglects or willfully withholds pay that corresponds to the quality and quantity of the service a person renders it. The Law of Compensation often works quietly and unnoticed except by the person who is attuned to hear its silent message. The wise person neither doubts the existence of, nor pranks with, the Law of Compensation. They make their conduct conform to its nature, thereby harnessing it to their purpose in life.

THE MAGIC KEY

There is a great Magic Key that unlocks the door to the human heart and gains welcome admittance for all who use it.

This great key, if it were universally used, would make wars impossible.

It would take away all desire to defraud a brother out of that which is his.

It would unlock the door to the storehouse of all knowledge and show us the peace and joy and happiness and success that come from understanding the human heart.

It would insure us supreme happiness.

It would insure us all of life's necessities and as many of the luxuries as we cared to indulge in.

And, what is this Great Magic Key?

It is the Golden Rule.

If we all understood the law back of the Golden Rule, we would see the necessity of becoming our brother's keeper. Strikes and lockouts would be absurdities that no civilized country would tolerate. Profiteering would bring swift failure to all who were foolish enough to undertake it.

If you want to know what is just and fair in your dealings with your neighbors, reverse every situation which you are about to create for the other person and see yourself in his place. If you would not be delighted to take their place and let them take yours, you may be sure the transaction does not square up with the Golden Rule.

You may be sure, also, that sooner or later, the eternal scales will be balanced and you, yourself, will stand in exactly the same situation that you created for your fellow man.

FRIENDS PROVE FALSE

No matter how many friends prove false and thereby strike a blow at your confidence in others, there is always one person to whom you can turn for consolation in hours of trial and disappointment.

You may see this person by stepping to the looking glass.

And, after all has been said and done, there is no one on whom you need to rely and who is more able to help you than yourself. It may serve as an alibi if you blame your failures on others, but the truth will remain that you, yourself, are responsible for your advancement or lack of it, and you are indeed fortunate if you get this consciousness and, henceforth, hold yourself accountable for your condition in life.

Make excuses for the shortcomings of OTHERS, but hold YOURSELF to strict accountability if you would attain leadership in any undertaking.

NOT HIS JOB!

"I'm not supposed to do that," said he,
When an extra task he chanced to see;
"That's not my job, and it's not my care,
So I'll pass it by and I'll leave it there."
And the boss who gave him his weekly pay
Lost more than his wages on him that day.
"I'm not supposed to do that," hesaid;
"That duty belongs to Jim or Fred."
So a little task that was in his way
That he could have handled without delay
Was left unfinished; the way was paved
For a heavy loss that he could have saved.
And time went on and he kept his place
But he never altered his easy pace,
And folks remarked on how well he knew
The line of the tasks he was hired to do;
For never once was he known to turn
His hand to things not of his concern.
But there in his foolish rut he stayed
And for all he did he was fairly paid,
But he never was worth a dollar more
Than he got for his toil when the week was o'er;
For he knew too well when his work was through
And he'd done all he was hired to do.
If you want to grow in this world, young man,
You must do every day all the work you can;
If you find a task, though it's not your bit,
And it should be done, take care of it!
And you'll never conquer or rise if you
Do only the things you're supposed to do.

OPPORTUNITY

Never in the history of the world has opportunity been so abundant as
it is now.

We have learned that people are limited only by their own lack of self-confidence and faith in humanity.

The way in which nature has yielded up her secrets to mankind during these past twenty years has proved that we can accomplish much when we learn to expect much of ourselves.

We have been taught the folly of strife and revenge and the virtue of cooperative effort. The World War taught us that the winner is also the loser when people engage in any sort of destructive effort.

With all these great lessons which we have learned, we stand face to face, now, with the opportunity to *impose* the sum total of what we have learned upon the minds of our children so that it may become a part of their philosophy and lead the next generation to heights of attainment that will startle the world.

This is the only method through which we can pass on to posterity the benefit of that which we have learned through combat, struggle, and experimentation. What a glorious opportunity now awaits the leadership of people in the schools, churches, and the public press, the three leading mediums through which these great lessons can be firmly planted in the minds of our youth.

Those who see this opportunity and have the initiative and the courage to embrace it may sweep on to fame and fortune on the wings of a powerful force that has arisen out of the agitation, strife, and chaos of the past seven years.

Let us all contribute our individual support and cooperation to the end that our children may be taught the advantages of placing principle above the dollar, and humanity, as a whole, above the individual.

ORGANIZED EFFORT

Out of organized effort comes power. There is an enormous amount of power in the raindrops, but it is merely potential until the raindrops are poured over a Niagara Falls or a mill wheel, or expanded in a steam boiler, in organized fashion.

There is power in your brain, but it is merely potential until it is organized, through the coordination of your faculties, and directed toward the achievement of a definite aim.

On every hand, nature sets us a fine example of the necessity of organization. Every blade of grass and every insect and every animal and every star visible to the human eye offers a marvelous specimen of organized effort of the highest order.

Every successful person has succeeded through the operation of this principle of organized effort. Carnegie accumulated millions through its use, and, contrary to the general belief, he made his millions out of organizing brains instead of steel. The steel business was but an incident in his financial success. He could have done as well in the cotton business. An organized mind can succeed in any undertaking.

The formula for success is as definable and as definite as are the rules of mathematics, and the very warp and woof of this formula is organized effort. The person who has learned to avail themselves of the power of organized effort always takes advantage of the accumulated facts bearing on the object of his definite aim or the work at hand for the moment. They delve into the libraries and laboratories and informs themselves of all that other people have learned about a given subject. This is one of the first and most essential steps to be taken by all who would make use of the power of organized effort.

THE PENALTY OF LEADERSHIP

In every field of human endeavor, there are people who are must perpetually live in the white light of publicity. Whether the leadership be vested in a person or in a manufactured product, emulation and envy are ever at work.

In art, in literature, in music, in industry, the reward and the punishment are always the same.

The reward is widespread recognition; the punishment is fierce denial and detraction.

When a person's work becomes a standard for the whole world, it also becomes a target for the shafts of the envious few. If their work be merely mediocre, they will be left severely alone—if they achieve a masterpiece, it will set a million tongues a-wagging.

Jealousy does not protrude its forked tongue at the artist who produces a commonplace painting.

Whatsoever you write, or paint, or play, or sing, or build, no one will strive to surpass or slander you, unless your work be stamped with the seal of genius.

Long, long after a great work or a good work has been done, those who are disappointed or envious continue to cry out that it cannot be done.

Spiteful little voices in the domain of art were raised against our own Whistler as a mountebank, long after the big world has acclaimed him its greatest artistic genius. The leader is assailed because they are a leader, and the effort to equal them is merely added proof of that leadership.

Failing to equal or to excel, the follower seeks to depreciate and to destroy—but only confirms the superiority of that which they strive to supplant.

There is nothing new in this.

It is as old as the world and as old as the human passions—envy, fear, greed, ambition, and the desire to surpass.

And it all avails nothing.

If the leader truly leads, they remain—the leader.

Master-poet, master-painter, master-workman, each in his turn is assailed, and each holds his laurels through the ages.

That which is good or great makes itself known, no matter how loud the clamor of denial.

That which deserves to live—lives.

SERVICE

If you serve an ungrateful master, serve him the more. Put God in your debt. Every stroke shall be repaid. The longer the payment is withheld, the better for you; for compound interest on compound interest is the rate and usage in this exchequer.—Emerson

Out of resistance comes strength; therefore, render the best service of which you are capable, regardless of the monetary compensation you are receiving for your efforts.

What you want is power, and this comes by organizing and exercising all of your faculties to the limit, just as an arm grows strong out of constant use.

Never mind about the pay. Take a lesson from the farmer who plows his ground, fertilizes it, plants the seed, and then waits for the reaction which is sure to provide him with a rich harvest.

Plant the seed of service that is right in quality and quantity, then watch what happens when you have established the reputation of being a person who always renders better service than that which is paid for.

If you will form the habit of rendering more service and better service than that which you contract to perform, very soon the law of increasing returns will begin to work in your favor, you will profit by contrast, and your harvest time will have come, for you will be eagerly sought and willingly paid for more than you actually do.

SOCIAL HEREDITY

All thought of wars and racial and religious antagonism and hatred and bigotry and world domination and injustice can be swept away in one generation.

If this is true, it renders a powerful indictment against our boasted civilization.

How, and by whom, can this "miracle" be performed?

It can be brought about through the combined efforts of the leaders, the schools, and the public press who have it within their power to force an ideal upon the minds of the young, which would lift the human race above its present vicious tendencies, and show us the advantage to all of placing humanity above the individual.

In one generation, these leaders, through the aid of the principle of social heredity, could sweep away every cause for antagonism between people by imposing on the minds of the young the ideal of subordination of the individual to the common welfare of organized humanity.

Japan has achieved the greatest miracle in modern times, through the aid of this principle of social heredity, by imposing an ideal upon the minds of her young. Through this principle, she has taught her young to subordinate the interest of the individual to the common aims of the nation as a whole, thereby transforming herself, in a few decades, into a potential power for good or evil which has eclipsed that of Ancient Rome.

Boastful civilization, stop, look, and reason.

SOLITUDE

Get away from the crowds, relax, quit the business of thinking, and give the genius within you a chance to express itself. Thirty minutes a day devoted to relaxation will give you poise and self-control, without which you can never become a master in any undertaking.

There is something in the calm stillness of nature which gives one faith, courage, and self-confidence. Go out into the woods, away from everybody, and give the subtle forces of nature a chance to lay hold on you.

In the solitude of your own heart, during these visits with your inner self, you will learn who you are and what your mission in life is.

Milton did his greatest work after blindness forced him to seek his inner self as a companion. Helen Keller has become the marvel of this age because she was deprived of the senses of sight, hearing, and speech and was forced to seek companionship with her inner self.

The connecting link between you and God may be found within your own heart, and nowhere else. There is a secret passageway between you and mastery, and it can be discovered only through that calm sereneness of thought which will flow in on you when you are alone, relaxed, and receptive.

This is no mere preachment, but a scientific truth, which, if studied and applied, may lead you upward to the heights of your desires.

STOP, LOOK, AND REASON

Don't be too hard on the person who has made a mistake. If the truth were known, it might disclose the fact that you, or your father, or your father's father would have been in a "helluva" fix if judged by a single act. Nearly everybody makes mistakes, and the person who disclaims having made one, confesses at the same time to never having achieved anything worth mentioning. I never see one person trying to disclose the scarlet letter on another's breast that I do not wonder if they don't carry some mark of disgrace which would have ruined them for life, and justice overtaken them. Every time I think about showing someone up or tearing someone down, I go out by myself and read Emerson's essay on "Compensation" again, for I know I need another injection of the truth it teaches. You might profit by the same procedure.

THANKS

I am thankful that I was born poor, that I did not come into this world burdened by the whims of wealthy parents, with a bag of gold around my neck.

I am thankful for the adversities which have crossed my pathway, for they have taught me self-control, perseverance, tolerance, and forgiveness.

I am thankful for the mistakes I have made, for through them, I have learned the wisdom of caution.

I am thankful for having discovered that only that which I do for myself will be of permanent benefit to me.

I am thankful for having learned that I may enjoy real happiness in exact proportion to the extent that I help others to be happy.

I ENTREPRENEUR TIP

Need to take a beat and remember what got you here? Try keeping a gratitude journal, where you can remind yourself each day of what you are thankful for.

I am thankful for having learned that before I can GET, I must GIVE, and that I will get exactly that which I give.

I am thankful for having learned that the best way to punish those who are unjust toward me is not to punish them at all, except by practicing the Golden Rule philosophy.

I am thankful for having learned, from the World War that has just closed, that brute force of might cannot win against that greater force of right, and that this applies to an individual the same as to nations.

I am thankful for having learned the folly of engaging in any transaction which does not benefit all who participate.

I am thankful for having learned that "like attracts like" and that "Whatsoever a person soweth, that shall they also reap."

THIS I RESOLVE TO DO

A person, being of sound health and disposing mind, hereby can set down these things that they have *resolved*: I will profit by the experience of others and will not wait to learn sense by my own experience. I will be teachable. From every human being I encounter, I will learn something. I will decide by my intellect what my tastes ought to be and make myself like the right things. I will put away the weakling's argument that, "I can't help my likes and dislikes."

I will keep clean in body and mind. I will not accept as a satisfactory standard what the majority of people are and do. I will allow no person nor institution to coerce my opinion; my judgment shall remain unterrified, unbribed, unseduced. In this I will not be truculent and offensive, but modest and open to conviction. I will not declare my belief in anything social or scientific that I do not clearly understand. *I will learn to do some one kind of work expertly, and make my living by that.* I will take from the world only the fair equivalent of what I give it. I will never take revenge, will harbor no grudges, and utterly eliminate any spirit of retaliation. Life is too short for destruction; all my efforts shall be constructive.

I will not engage in any business or sport that implies fraud, cruelty, or injustice to any living thing. I will hurt no child, punish no man, wrong no woman. In everything I do, I shall strive to add a little to the sum of happiness and subtract a little from the sum of misery of all living creatures. I will constantly try to make myself agreeable to all persons with whom I come in contact. I know death is as natural as birth, and that no person knows their hour. I will not fret at this, nor dodge it, but so live that I am ready to go. I will believe that honesty is better than crookedness, truth is better than lies, cleanliness is better than dirty, loyalty is better than treachery, and love is better than hate or coldness. I will trust my life and my career to an unfailing reliance upon this creed.

THIS, TOO, WILL SOON PASS

There will be days when you will be discouraged, then is the time to remember that no person is always fortunate; that the wheel of life is always turning, and when the flat side comes around, as it is sure to do some time, just remember that it will turn on by if you will wait without losing faith in yourself and in the divine hand that created you. Those experiences which discourage you may be nothing more than nature's plan for tempering you for some great work in life. While waiting for the trouble of the moment to pass may it not be well to think of Lincoln, the log cabin, and the White House, bearing in mind, meanwhile, that the White House is none too high a goal for which to aim.

TIME

Time is the only priceless treasure in the universe.

Time is the friend of all who are true unto themselves and who play the game of life squarely with humanity, but it is the mortal enemy of all who cheat and all who try to get without giving a fair equivalent.

Time heals wounded hearts, rebuilds lost faith, and eradicates hatred, envy, and jealousy. Time strikes the scales of ignorance from the eyes, and reveals to all who will see the beauty and glory and happiness that are born of wholesome love for humanity.

Time is the mighty hand that rocks the eternal cradle of progress and nurses struggling humanity through that period during which a person needs protection against their own ignorance.

Time softens the human heart and separates a person from their baser animal instincts. Fortunate is the person who learns, before the age of 40, the cleansing value of time.

Without the aid of Time, the Law of Compensation falls flat and becomes practically inoperative. Time is forever changing, tearing down, and rebuilding mankind; therefore, no person can be properly judged except they be weighed over a considerable period of time.

Character, good or bad, is the sum total of the handiwork of time, through the aid of which one's thoughts and actions have been slowly woven into character. Time builds character out of whatever it finds to work with, but never goes outside of one's own thoughts and actions for material.

Time compensates the human race for all its virtues and exacts appropriate penalties for all its mistakes. That which it doesn't pay back to or exact from the individual, it hands back to or collects from the community.

TIME, THE GREATEST TEACHER

Who has not approached the afternoon of life without having seen evidence that Time is a faultless teacher to all who seek the truth? The great tragedy of life is not that we must die, but that we too often die at the time when truth and the possibilities of life are just beginning to unfold themselves to us.

Time is a wonderful teacher. If we give it a chance, it will unfold to us all the truth we need as we journey by the wayside of life.

Among other truths which Time brings us, are these:

Happiness, the ultimate object of every human heart, can come only by helping others find it.

Strength comes out of struggle and disappointment and defeat and the mastery of obstacles which beset our pathway.

It pays to render more service and better service than one is paid to render, because this practice develops strength of character and attracts to us the choicest of people who seek to ally themselves with us.

By winding or straight roads, our own thoughts and acts toward others come back to bless or to curse us; we reap that which we sow. The slanderer is, in due time, destroyed by the vileness of his own tongue.

Enemies are a valuable asset to the person who is big enough and tolerant enough to smile at their attempts to destroy them because of the fact that they know that time is always the friend of the person who is right and the enemy of the person who is wrong.

Every effect corresponds in nature to its cause, which guarantees proper reward to the person whose fundamental principles in life are built upon the Golden Rule and whose philosophy is that of constructive service for the good of humanity.

The laws of success are as determinable and as workable and as sure of the same results, when correctly applied, in every transaction as are the rules of mathematics.

A person's character is the sum total of their dominating thoughts.

Thought is the most highly organized form of energy known to humans and transcends, in importance, all other forms of organized effort and all physical matter.

Dishonesty, in any form whatsoever, is destructive and dangerous, not because the one practicing it may be found out by others and punished, but because of its disintegrating effect on themselves. Dishonesty causes loss of self-respect which, in turn, attracts the negative qualities that lead to failure and defeat.

Truth and justice must be the foundation upon which every transaction is based or else the results of the transaction cannot endure. Nowhere do we find nature favoring falsehood or injustice.

We grow to resemble the environment in which we exist and to conform to the philosophy of those with whom we associate most closely, which makes it possible for us to change our character by changing our environment.

Out of every failure, we may learn a great lesson, regardless of the cause of the failure, whether within our control or outside of it.

ULTIMATELY NOTHING MATTERS

At some point in my journey through life, I picked up a bit of stray philosophy that has come to my rescue on many occasions when days seemed dark and everything seemed to go dead wrong.

It may be stated in these word: "Ultimately, nothing matters; therefore, why worry about anything?"

Looking back over the past 20 odd years by which I measure my business experience, I can see that the obstacles ahead of me which resembled impassable mountains turned out go be nothing but molehills.

The trouble which I worried about seldom materialized. Seven different times, I went down in defeat, yet I now know that I came up stronger and wiser at each of those seven rough turning points of my life.

As I write these lines, I have before me a check from Bernard McFadden, of the Physical Culture Corporation, for $300. That check is in payment of my services for less than two hours' time, yet, it really was in payment for work I did as a result of something I learned during those seven turning points which I once called failures.

napoleon hill's first editions

Last night, I delivered a lecture (the Magic Ladder to Success) before the employees of a large corporation. After the lecture, the president handed me his personal check for $500. The material out of which that lecture was created came from the failures I experienced over a period of practically 20 years, and I am reminded, now, that each of those failures looked like my finish at the time.

Today, I was honored by a group of well-known scientific people who elected me President of the National Chiropractic Sanitarium, thus placing me in charge of a corporation that aims to build a chain of sanitariums in the leading cities of America. Upon slight analysis of the reason for my having been honored by these men, I am reminded that it was because of what I have learned of organized effort and of leadership, most of which I gathered from what I once called failure, at the seven turning points of my life.

If I had the space, I could enumerate more than a score of incidents, each of which would prove that, out of failures, we may build success, providing we do not look upon failure as being anything except a necessary teacher. Every one of these incidents would prove that no person should worry about anything.

It may be a mere coincidence, but the fact remains that this little bit of philosophy, "ultimately nothing matters," marked the turning point in my life at which I began to smile at failures. When I began to smile instead of frown at them, they became fewer and fewer, and before very long, the lessons I had learned from them began to lead me towards the heights of my desires.

What if a friend does prove false? What if you do lose your fortune—do you not understand that your real wealth lies within your brain and your capacity to serve, and not in the vaults of a bank?

When you face a situation that is embarrassing and you feel old person worry laying his chilly hands upon you, just remember that they can scare you only with your consent, not without it. It is within your power to shield your heart from the sharp blows of worry, fear, and despair, and you can do this by keeping in mind the fact that "ultimately nothing matters."

This philosophy has brought me poise and a calmness which I never knew before, and in the very stillness of this poise, I have been able to hear the voice of one whose voice I had never heard before, a voice that guides me to the heights which I never could have reached alone. "Ultimately nothing matters."

THE WHISTLING POSTMAN

EDITOR'S NOTE: *This piece is an example of how Hill uses storytelling to make a point. Here, he is telling the reader to not despair when things seem impossible. Instead, live your life as it comes rather than accepting suffering and misery now in the hopes of a payoff later. Everything that comes your way in life—or in business—is useful.*

As we journey by the wayside of life, let us not forget that we can take nothing with us when the Great Caravan draws up and taps us on the shoulder; therefore, let us spread sunshine and happiness while we are here, that it may illuminate the pathway of some weary traveler.

As he steps off the elevator just outside my office door, he begins to whistle some old, well-known melody.

I catch the rhythm of his tune, and I whistle as I write these lines. My stenographer catches the rhythm of my tune, and she blends it with her work, and I doubt not that the readers of this magazine catch the rhythm as they read.

He is a humble postman, earning his living by carrying a heavy pack on his shoulder from morning until night, yet he is rendering a far-reaching service by whistling instead of cursing the fate which makes it necessary for him to carry letters for a living.

Credit him with these lines because he inspired me to write them. And, if you have a mind that turns now and then toward the philosophy of life and seeks the cause for happiness and sorrow, follow this thought back to its cause and analyze it.

More than 100,000 people will read this story of the Whistling Postman, and some of them, including yourself we hope, will pick up the thought back of it and spread it broadcast.

This morning, black clouds shut off the sunshine, and a drizzling rain cast a dampening effect over our entire office force until we heard the Whistling Postman step off the elevator as he whistled "Pack Up Your Troubles In Your Old Kit Bag and Smile, Smile, Smile!" Everybody smiled. As he disappeared down the long hallways, we could hear the echo of his tune as it grew softer and softer.

How many souls this Postman gladdens as he makes his rounds each day, I do not know, but I do know that he leaves our office full of good cheer. He inspires us all to serve the readers of this magazine better than we would do if he greeted us with a snarl in his voice, or not at all. And we, in turn, to some extent inspire our readers to emulate the Whistling Postman.

What a pity we have not more Whistling Postmen and Whistling Butchers and Whistling Stenographers and Whistling Employers and Whistling Strangers on the streets. No one can whistle one of the sweet old melodies and, at the same time, hold hatred and distrust and destructive thoughts in his mind. The two will not mix.

This old world can stand a number of Whistling Postmen right now, but as far as we are able to interpret the needs of the times, we have no use for the grouch or the cynic. Let's all whistle for a change. Perhaps it is a bit undignified—well, well, what of that?

Whistle up, old skate, you good-natured old duffer! It might cure your indigestion and save your job or your business.

WORK

All external good has its tax, and if it came without desert of sweat, has no root in me, and the next wind will blow it away—Emerson

Legislate as ye may, devise as ye please, dream as ye will, become fanatical on some particular "ism" that is soon to usher in the millennium, grow wild-eyed over the rainbows that fill a Bolshevik sky, concoct all the grand schemes for the solution of our social and industrial ills that the freedom of our country will allow, and your unbridled imaginations can conceive, *and*, when your fever shall have burned itself out; when you again have a normal appetite for food; when you can sleep once more without seeing visions, you will awake to a never-varying realization that, throughout all the tide of time, as long as person is possessed of a physical body, is fired by the ambitions of leadership and of service, feels wild passions beating in their blood, is keenly conscious of the progressive urge of the ages, sees in the far-off tomorrow the resplendent beauty of better days whose glories are yet to fill the world, aspires to a spiritual imminence which will free them from the shackles of cold materialism—as long as a person shall live and love—the fruition of all the theories for the division of things material, the realization of all dreams *will never yield a substitute for work!*

YOU CAN DO IT

Unless you are one of that small minority of human beings whose positive, self-reliant attitude toward life makes it unnecessary for them to be encouraged and who need no refuge in moments of distress, you will be wise if you cultivate some person who will take you by the shoulder in a kindly sort of way and say, "You can do it!"

If you visited the New York office of this magazine, you would be greeted with these four words the moment you stepped into the elevator, where they hang on a neatly framed card.

When you stepped off the elevator, you would be greeted with the same words on the front door.

As you entered the reception room, you would see those words on every door to the private offices, and unless you happened to be in an unusually bad humor, you would be apt to feel the psychology of those words taking hold of you and filling you with belief in yourself.

If you stepped into the washroom of the offices, you would see those same words on the mirror. You would find no other lettering of any sort on any of our doors. On the desk of every stenographer, you would see these "YOU CAN DO IT" cards, and you would find one of them as the only adornment of the editor's private desk.

Perhaps you would get the impression that those "YOU CAN DO IT" signs were designed for the benefit of those who visit our offices, but they were not; they were created for the psychological effect they have on those who work in our offices, from the editor on down to the office boy.

That which we all need, more or less, is self-confidence in abundance. Suggestion is a powerful factor in the development of self-confidence, and we all need such suggestion. These "YOU CAN DO IT" signs are working wonders in our offices. They remind us, constantly, that we demand self-reliance.

From this time on, you will see these four words on every magazine published by the Hill Publishing Trust, including *Napoleon Hill's Magazine*. You will see these words on practically every letterhead that leaves our offices, and you will see them on the outside of every envelope. Very soon, you will see these four words on neatly designed cards, printed in colors, on the walls of every office you visit because we have made up such cards for free distribution to all who ask for them.

This is a "YOU CAN DO IT" age in which we are living and we want the whole of America to catch the thought and be guided by it. The editor is preparing to have a radio station installed in his office, through the aid of which he can speak to an audience of more than 15 million people every Sunday afternoon, for the purpose of rendering them a service that will supplement the work being done through his pen. His decision to provide this additional means of serving came as a result of the "YOU CAN DO IT" sign that looks up at him from under the plate glass top on his desk and smiles out at him as he walks into his office.

These "YOU CAN DO IT" signs were installed in our office only a week ago, yet everyone here has caught the spirit of them, and it is manifesting itself in the quality and quantity of work we are performing. Write for one of these "YOU CAN DO IT" cards and place it where it can work for you, quietly, silently, and subtly.

You can do it!

THE BEST-LIKED PERSON

You can make yourself the best-liked person on the works by having something friendly to say to everyone to whom you speak. You can become the best-liked person in your neighborhood by the same method. Incidentally, this plan will not detract anything from your pay envelope; it might add something to it. Give the plan a trial for one week, and you will know why you ought to use it permanently.

/ ENTREPRENEUR TIP

Positivity is a hallmark of Hill's philosophy. Why not make it a part of yours? Even on your worst day, if you can focus your energies on sending out positive thoughts and words to your coworkers and colleagues, you can enhance your own outlook in the process.

CHARACTER BUILDING

You are constantly building your character out of the impressions you gather from your daily environment; therefore, you can shape your character as you wish. If you would build it strongly, surround yourself with the pictures of the great people you most admire; hang mottoes of positive affirmation on the walls of your room; place the books of your favorite authors on the table where you can get at them often, and read those books with pencil in hand, marking the lines which bring you the noblest thoughts; fill your mind with the biggest and noblest and most elevating thoughts, and soon you will begin to see your own character taking on the hue and color of this environment which you have created for yourself.

YOUR DEFINITE AIM IN LIFE

This is the time of year when good resolutions are in order; therefore, you may find it profitable to turn down this page and come back to it again, for it brings a thought that 95 percent of the people of the world need.

There is a law through the operation of which thought is transformed into action and action into concrete, physical form in the shape of those worldly goods and wares which most people are trying to accumulate.

May I not give you the simple formula through which you may avail yourself of the power of this law?

Write on the front page of a small blank book a clear, concise statement of your Definite Aim in Life. The words in which you write this statement are not important, nor does it make any difference how any or how few words you use as long as you make your statement *definite*.

At another place in the book, begin writing out a *definite* plan for attaining your *definite* aim, and add to this plan from day to day until you are satisfied that it is both practical and complete.

Then read both your Definite Aim and your Plan for attaining it every night, just before going to sleep, and at least once a day, at the most convenient time. As you read, be sure to *have faith* in your ability to attain your aim through the plan which you have created for its attainment.

To make sure that you will have this faith, which is as necessary as is the plan and the aim itself, read or affirm the aim, as you have it written out in your book, as though it were a prayer.

If you have faith, this procedure can bring you nothing but *success*!

I am in position to assure you that this plan cannot fail if the object of your *aim* is just and right and does not inflict hardship or disadvantage on others; therefore, observe the Golden Rule in creating your Aim and your Plan for attaining it, and success will be yours just as sure as the sun goes to sleep in the West and awakes in the East the next morning.

You can make this year the banner year of your life if you will adopt this simple Plan and persistently and faithfully carry it out for six months.

You cannot fail because you will have formed an alliance with a power that knows no resistance!

YOUR OWN WILL COME TO YOU

Every proverb, every book, every byword that belongs to thee for aid or comfort shall surely come home through open or winding passages. Every friend whom not thy fantastic will but the great and tender heart in thee craveth, shall lock thee in his embrace.—Emerson

The law of attraction will cause all that harmonizes with your personality to gravitate to you, as steel filings are attracted to a magnet. There is no escape from this law; therefore, build the Golden Rule into your personality if you would insure against regrets.

A Reader's Guide to *Napoleon Hill's First Editions*

From advice on habits to meditations on mindfulness, the passages featured in *Napoleon Hill's First Editions* share some of Hill's most evergreen advice on success with you. As you've likely noticed, these classic writings on what creates, supports, and sustains success all approach the topic differently. But one narrative thread connects them all in a tapestry that gives you, the reader, a comprehensive roadmap to success: the thread of personal development. What makes you successful is . . . you. And you are the architect of your own success story.

Now, you can start to apply those lessons to your own journey. To help you do that, the editors at *Entrepreneur* have designed a reader's guide that will help you revisit the stories, anecdotes, and lessons from Napoleon Hill's first published writings and think about them more deeply. The discussion questions below are designed to help you identify what speaks to you most in this book while, at the same time, help you identify what is most important to you about your own success journey. Feel free to use these discussion questions not just once, but often, as you move toward your own goals. Why often? Because everyone's mileage may vary on the journey to success. What is important to you today may be replaced by a new goal, idea, or priority down the road. That's why the lessons here are timeless, and these questions are created to travel with you every step of the way.

DISCUSSION QUESTIONS

- What concept of Hill's speaks to you the most at this particular moment in time?
- What advice can you apply to your own journey right now? Do you envision your answer changing over time? How about in the next year, or five years?
- Does Hill's take on the Golden Rule speaks to your own experiences? Why?
- If you could identify three key takeaways from each essay, what would they be? How do they apply to your own success journey?
- What is your favorite quote or concept in this book? Why?
- As you begin to see yourself and your own journey reflected in these essays, think about advice you've gotten over the years. Do any of the suggestions or concepts in this book remind you of success strategies you've heard in your own life? If so, how?
- Share some favorite quotes from the book with someone you interact with on your own success journey. How you can you explain those quotes to a mentee or someone who has coached or mentored you?
- If you could have a personal chat with Napoleon Hill, what would you ask him?
- If you could take any of the essays here and put your own spin on it, what would you change? How would you help apply lessons from

your own life to Hill's anecdotes?

- What is something you learned in this book that you didn't already know?
- Do any of the essays spark new questions for you about your own success journey? What are they?
- What advice in the book is most relatable to you? The least? Why?
- What common themes do you see running through the essays?
- How do those common themes apply to you?
- If you wrote your own essay on success, habits, or personal development, what would it be about? Would that topic change over time?
- Think about your five-year and ten-year goals. Where do you want to be? What do you want to be doing? If you could assign your future self an essay to read based on those goals, what would it be? Why?

Resources

The Entrepreneur Action Items sections that accompany each selection are derived from articles and content originally appearing on entrepreneur.com. They include:

"The Golden Rule is Just as Good for Businesses As It Is For People" by Melissa Powell, https://www.entrepreneur.com/article/304430

"8 Ways to Stay Accountable With Your Goals" by Deep Patel, https://www.entrepreneur.com/article/328070

"5 Ways to Rekindle Your Passion for Leadership" by Richard Trevino II, https://www.entrepreneur.com/article/346158

"Use These 7 Emotional Intelligence Tips to Be a Better Leader" by John Boitnott, https://www.entrepreneur.com/article/304206

"5 Steps for Bouncing Back After You Fail" by Jolie Dawn, https://www.entrepreneur.com/article/319607

"10 Essential Qualities for Living an Authentically Empowered Life" by Sherrie Campbell, https://www.entrepreneur.com/article/295137

"6 Ways Well-Organized People Get More Done Every Day" by John

Rampton, https://www.entrepreneur.com/article/299034

"Why Emotional Intelligence Can Make or Break Your Organization" by Caroline Stokes, https://www.entrepreneur.com/article/334872

"How to Take a Personal Stake in Your Employees' Development" by Tiffany Delmore, https://www.entrepreneur.com/article/340661

"12 Things First-Time Leaders Need to Succeed" by Angela Kambouris, https://www.entrepreneur.com/article/343572

"12 Self-Awareness Exercises That Fuel Success" by Thai Nguyen, https://www.entrepreneur.com/article/254669

About Napoleon Hill

Napoleon Hill was born in 1883 in a one-room cabin on the Pound River in Wise County, Virginia. He began his writing career at age 13 as a "mountain reporter" for small-town newspapers and went on to become America's most beloved motivational author. Hill passed away in November 1970 after a long and successful career writing, teaching, and lecturing about the principles of success.

Dr. Hill's work stands as a monument to individual achievement and is the cornerstone of modern motivation. His book, *Think and Grow Rich*, is the all-time bestseller in the field. Hill established the Napoleon Hill Foundation as a nonprofit educational institution whose mission is to perpetuate his philosophy of leadership, self-motivation, and individual achievement. Learn more about Napoleon Hill at www.naphill.org.

Index